Learning Grows

Learning Grows

The Science of Motivation for the Classroom Teacher

Andrew C. Watson

ROWMAN & LITTLEFIELD
Lanham • Boulder • New York • London

Published by Rowman & Littlefield
An imprint of The Rowman & Littlefield Publishing Group, Inc.
4501 Forbes Boulevard, Suite 200, Lanham, Maryland 20706
www.rowman.com

6 Tinworth Street, London, SE11 5AL, United Kingdom

Copyright © 2019 by Andrew C. Watson

All figures created by author unless otherwise noted.

All rights reserved. No part of this book may be reproduced in any form or by any electronic or mechanical means, including information storage and retrieval systems, without written permission from the publisher, except by a reviewer who may quote passages in a review.

British Library Cataloguing in Publication Information Available

Library of Congress Cataloging-in-Publication Data

Names: Watson, Andrew C., author.
Title: Learning grows : the science of motivation for the classroom teacher / Andrew C. Watson.
Description: Lanham, Maryland : Rowman & Littlefield, [2019] | Series: A teacher's guide to the learning brain series | Includes bibliographical references and index.
Identifiers: LCCN 2018058891 (print) | LCCN 2019007540 (ebook) | ISBN 9781475833355 (Electronic) | ISBN 9781475833331 (cloth : alk. paper) | ISBN 9781475833348 (pbk. : alk. paper)
Subjects: LCSH: Motivation in education. | Learning, Psychology of. | Cognitive neuroscience.
Classification: LCC LB1065 (ebook) | LCC LB1065 .W366 2019 (print) | DDC 370.15/4—dc23
LC record available at https://lccn.loc.gov/2018058891

∞™ The paper used in this publication meets the minimum requirements of American National Standard for Information Sciences—Permanence of Paper for Printed Library Materials, ANSI/NISO Z39.48-1992.

Printed in the United States of America

To Cody, Lucy, Kaylee, and Brady,
my four favorite learners.

And to H3,
my favorite.

Contents

About A Teacher's Guide to the Learning Brain Series ... ix
Preface ... xi
Introduction ... xv

PART I: MINDSET

1 Starting at the Fourth Step ... 3
2 Second Step: Rehearsing, Not Performing ... 31
3 The First Step (at Last) ... 47
4 The Mindset Controversy and FAQs ... 71

PART II: STEREOTYPE THREAT

5 (De)Motivation and Stereotypes ... 85
6 Changing the Motivational Climate ... 111
7 Assessment and Stereotype Threat FAQs ... 127

References ... 143
Index ... 151
About the Author ... 153

About A Teacher's Guide to the Learning Brain Series

In the twenty-first century, teachers have increasingly turned to brain scientists—psychologists and neuroscientists—to understand how students learn. This emerging field of Mind, Brain, and Education weaves together the practical know-how of classroom teachers and the scientific knowledge of scholars.

A Teacher's Guide to the Learning Brain series brings together the most important conclusions of this transdisciplinary work, exploring its best-researched and most useful conclusions. By explaining psychology and neuroscience with clarity and humor, and by illuminating research conclusions with real-world classroom examples, this series helps teachers make learning easier and teaching more effective.

The first book, *Learning Begins*, considers the science of *working memory* and of *attention*. In this volume, teachers learn how students integrate new knowledge and new skills with their current memory systems. By exploring the surprising complexity of human attentional systems, teachers also learn how to help students focus on essential learning goals.

The second book, *Learning Grows*, explores two essential theories of student *motivation*. Although science struggles to understand academic motivation, psychologists have much clearer ideas about classroom *demotivation*. When teachers convert a demotivating fixed mindset to a growth mindset, we help students learn and grow. Likewise, Claude Steele's theory of stereotype threat guides us in dismantling social forces that demotivate learners.

The final book, *Learning Thrives*, studies the formation of *long-term memories*—both in the brain (as new neural networks) and in the mind (as new learning). Teachers who understand the specific processes that encode, consolidate, and retrieve new memories can help students change their brains and change their minds.

Taken together, A Teacher's Guide to the Learning Brain series makes Mind, Brain, and Education clear, exciting, and useful for classroom teachers.

Preface

Part I of *Learning Grows* explores the rich and intricate development of mindset theory.

This theory holds an unusual place in schools. On the one hand, most teachers have heard of it; many have read about it and even tried out some of its suggestions.

On the other hand, most of what we "know" about mindset is worryingly incomplete. Some is outright incorrect.

For these reasons, part I takes an unusual approach, tracking mindset's step-by-step development over four decades. This historical perspective helps shift our focus from its final, shiny incarnation to the gritty classroom problems that prompted the research in the first place. Beneath the familiar surface, we'll find lots of surprising new perspectives.

Chapter 1 introduces the vexing classroom problem that got mindset research started.

When teachers plan our lessons, we know our students will spend some time being confused, perhaps frustrated. Their struggle might, on occasion, even feel like failure. Cognitive scientists even tell us that their struggle is good news: it promotes ultimate learning. Yet *motivation* researchers point out the bad news: such struggles can—in fact, often do—demotivate a substantial percentage of our students. Researchers routinely find that, while some students do *charge* in response to struggle, others simply *retreat*.

To motivate our students, then, we don't need to hype them up with pom-poms. Instead, we want to convert *retreat-prone* students into *charge-prone* students. When we succeed, they find intrinsic motivation in the mini-challenges that schooling automatically provides.

How, then, can we bring about this conversion? Chapter 1 explores one answer: we can help students understand their shortfalls not as a lack of ability but as a lack of strategic effort. This framework helps convert potential retreaters into chargers. Happily, psychologists have developed several research-informed strategies to do exactly that.

Chapter 2 offers a second set of conversion strategies. Like students' *explanations for struggle*, their *goals in school* can demotivate them. When teachers help students reject performance goals ("I must show you how much I know already!") and adopt learning goals ("Because I don't know everything, I'm here to learn new stuff"), we create a second motivational pathway that helps students charge. Here again, decades of research offer us classroom suggestions and techniques.

Chapter 3 arrives at the best-known part of this multi-layered motivation theory. Researcher Carol Dweck sought to understand why students had adopted these "charge" or "retreat" responses in the first place. She found that, at its foundation, students' motivation stems from their beliefs about intelligence. Those who think *intelligence can't change* get stuck in demotivating pathways. Those who believe *it can change*, by contrast, typically charge.

When teachers help students reject the first belief (which Dweck calls a "fixed mindset") and adopt the second (a "growth mindset"), we yet again help start a motivational cascade that encourages retreaters to become chargers. Like chapters 1 and 2, chapter 3 includes several research-supported strategies to bring about this transformation.

Because mindset theory has been developing for more than four decades, it has generated controversy along the way. In recent years, it has come under renewed scrutiny, especially because of the "replication crisis" in psychology. Chapter 4 looks at this controversy, exploring several arguments against mindset. Despite plausible doubts, we'll see that we have many reasons to remain confident. Especially because motivational theories are "elusive," we should be glad to have such a widely documented approach at hand.

Part II of *Learning Grows* turns to a more recent motivational theory: stereotype threat.

Less well-known than Dweck's work, this theory nonetheless has accumulated similar layers of misunderstanding. Because the core topic—stereotypes—is so stressful, it can distract us from the theory's true message. This research isn't trying to blame people; instead, it's trying to respond to social realities.

Happily, the strategies it suggests provide lots of ways to do so.

Chapter 5 explores the surprising forces that generate stereotype threat in the first place. Several paradoxical preconditions result in equally surprising (and counterproductive) responses. Those responses, in turn, tangle up essential parts of our students' cognitive apparatus: attention and working memory. Only by understanding this causal chain can teachers undo its pernicious effects.

The research that maps out this cause-and-effect process also teaches us how to prevent it. By focusing on the first step along the stereotype-threat path—"salience"—we can stop the whole system before it gets started. Chapter 6 reviews several strategies to create school climates that make stereotype threat substantially less likely. (Mindset theory makes a guest appearance in chapter 6 and will prove to be an important supporting player.)

Chapter 7 looks specifically at assessments, which by nature might invoke stereotype threat. Using a variety of strategies before, during, and after our tests, quizzes, and projects, we can again dispel the forces that impede student learning. Chapter 7 also includes two "bonus" strategies—ones that don't fit neatly into either previous category but nonetheless have enough research support to be worth exploring.

Taken together, parts I and II attempt to reshape conversations about motivation.

The word "motivation" comes from a Latin verb meaning "to move," and so it seems intuitive that charismatic energy ought to be required. We think of coaches enthralling players with heartfelt speeches and political leaders inspiring voters at get-out-the-vote rallies.

And yet, these two theories don't exactly *motivate* students. They require no cheer leaders, no chanting of slogans, no energetic waving of enthusiastic arms.

Instead, they confront and reduce the forces that *demotivate* students.

When teachers convert "fixed mindsets" to "growth mindsets," we remove vexing obstacles to learning. When we understand stereotype threat well enough to prevent it, we dismantle otherwise daunting roadblocks.

Seeing the path we have cleared for them—one free from obstacles and roadblocks—our students can go where their intrinsic motivation takes them. After all, as Willingham emphasizes, human beings like solvable puzzles (2009). We enjoy putting in mental effort and arriving at unexpected successes.

This new approach takes some getting used to. All this quiet, behind-the-scenes work to prevent demotivation doesn't seem as assertive as proactive motivation. However, unlike more rah-rah approaches, these theories have research behind them. And they're much less tiring to enact.

Parts I and II reshape conversations about motivation in a second way as well.

As we'll see below, mindset theory focuses primarily on *individual* accomplishment. Empowered by a growth mindset, each student sees new opportunities for personal success and new reasons for self-focused grit.

Stereotype threat, on the other hand, looks at *societal* forces within which students work. Because stereotypes exist—they really do—we should acknowledge and work to mitigate their influence. When we reshape school climates in very specific ways, we can create a social environment that fosters motivation.

A motivated (growth mindset) student working in a motivational (anti-stereotype-threat) environment has the best chance to succeed in school.

The cover of this book might deceive you into thinking that only one person wrote it. The truth defies that simple conclusion. My understanding of psychology and neuroscience, my ideas about classroom teaching, even my long-time fascination with learning all depend on people too numerous to count, much less name. I did write all the words in the book and organize its ideas. But in truth they were inspired, shaped, or carefully proofread by the people listed below. Because the theories I'll explain are somewhat controversial, I should emphasize that the errors and quirks that remain are my responsibility. Those thanked here do not necessarily endorse my conclusions. However, *Learning Grows* exists as it does because of their wisdom and support.

My thanks to: Pooja Agarwal, Alice Baxter, Maya Bialik, Tim Blesse, Sapna Cheryan, Tan Cher Chong, Joanna Christadoulou, Betsy Conger, Patty Cousins, Lisa Damour, David Daniel, Jeff and Jennifer Desjarlais, Mary Forrester, Kurt Fischer, Tina Grotzer, Paul L. Harris, Heath Hightower, Nancy Hill, Tyler Hodges, Marjorie Johnson, Sarah Jubar, Erik Kindblom, Nate Kornell, Dan LaGattuta, Gigi Luk, Scott MacClintic, Alec McCandless, Kevin Mattingly, Sara Mierke, Cindy Nebel, Elizabeth Parada, Judith Poirier, John Ratté, Todd Rose, Kim Samson, Stephanie Fine Sasse, Peter Scott, Lawrence Smith, Nick Soderstrom, Susan Tammaro, David Watson, Judy Watson, Peter Welch, Kelly Williams, Michael Wirtz, and Matt Young.

Introduction

Let's start with an urgent question: *what motivates our students?*

When teachers ponder this topic, we easily come up with a long list of answers.

- *Grades* motivate students.
- *Competition* motivates students.
- So does hunger. And boredom. (Well, boredom *demotivates* students.)
- A desire to impress that good-looking person over there provides lots of motivation.
- Parents motivate. Curiosity. Fidget spinners. Peers. Love of learning. *Fortnite*. Fear of failure. Projects. College aspirations. The pleasure of making progress. Surprises. Apps.
- Dinosaurs. *Dinosaurs* motivate students.

At the end of a long list, teachers occasionally admit that—well—*we* motivate students. Our students often like and admire us and want us to think well of them.

Here's the headline: *teachers already know a lot about motivation*. We took up teaching because we have a knack for inspiring students at a particular age. Second-grade teachers enjoy their work because, among other things, they know how to motivate second graders.

As we ponder our motivation question further, a newish interdisciplinary field might offer us wise guidance. Known as "Mind, Brain, and Education," this field creates conversations among teachers, psychologists, and neuroscientists. Because classroom teachers want to change our students' brains, we should have lots to learn from brain experts.

For example, the more we know about attention in the brain, the more we help our students focus in class. Scientific research can offer teachers practical guidance.

And yet, given how much teachers already know about motivation, we might doubt that Mind, Brain, and Education (MBE) experts have much to offer us here. Who knows more about practical motivation than we do?

At a minimum, if they want us to take their advice, this MBE guidance should meet at least two criteria.

- First: that advice should have *research* behind it. Teachers' experience, peers, and instincts have been helping us motivate students for years. We don't want psychologists and neuroscientists to have mere hypotheses. We want evidence. Reams of it.
- Second: MBE advice should be *surprising*, even *counterintuitive*. After all, we don't really need psychology research that tells us to do what we're already doing. That kind of research is nice, but—honestly—we don't need to read a book about it.

Truly useful research would challenge our instincts, give us new approaches to ponder, push our profession to try something new. Sadly, motivation researchers don't have much that fits this bill.

Even the editors of *American Psychologist* admit this problem, albeit rather tactfully: "Educationally relevant conceptions of motivation have been elusive" (Editorial, 1986, p. 1040). Elusive! This sounds like a polite way of saying: "Move along. Nothing for teachers to see here." Although teachers might be willing to hear from motivation experts, even the experts confess that they don't really have lots to tell us.

Despite this sheepish admission, the motivation cupboard is not utterly bare. Two powerful motivational theories from recent decades—mindset and stereotype threat—meet both of our criteria: lots of research support and usefully surprising suggestions.

Learning Grows delves into both these theories.

By the end of this book, you'll know how researchers developed their theories and how the pieces all fit together.

You'll know about the all-too-common misconceptions that badly oversimplify the first theory. You'll see how plausible misunderstandings frequently derail the second.

You'll know what skeptics have to say and why I still believe both theories can help us teach and students learn.

Most important, you'll have many (*many*) specific classroom examples. If you teach third grade or ninth, language arts or ceramics or earth sciences,

English Language Learners or Advanced Placement sections, project-based curricula or online classes—no matter what you teach, no matter whom you teach, you'll find guidance that readily translates to your teaching world.

At the same time that *Learning Grows* explains these two motivation theories, it also returns frequently to three essential MBE principles. While the theories offer teachers new ideas, the principles guide us in using them most effectively.

FIRST PRINCIPLE

When teachers attend brain conferences, we often hear specific, proscriptive messages. "When I did *this*," the researcher says, "my students learned more than when I did *that*." The implication is clear; in our classrooms, we too should do *this*, not *that*.

At times, the researcher's advice might usefully transfer directly from her lab to our classrooms.

However, MBE research more often helps us by *giving us new ways to think*. If we focus on the concepts underlying the researcher's suggested approach, we can apply them in our own way to our own circumstances.

Here's MBE principle #1: **Don't just *do this thing*; instead, *think this way*.**

For example, when Josh Aronson had college students write letters to imaginary middle-school pen pals, those letters helped the college students learn (Aronson, Fried, & Good, 2002). And yet teachers should not simply "do this thing." We should not, as Aronson did, deceive students about made-up seventh graders.

Instead, we should understand the idea behind Aronson's letters and apply that idea to our own classrooms. We should "think this way." Once we understand *why* Aronson had college students write those letters, we can quickly see how his technique will work for our students. No fictitious pen pals required.

SECOND PRINCIPLE

As we start "thinking this way," we will naturally start *adapting* researchers' strategies into our own teaching practices.

In one well-known study, Ying-Yi Hong had students read a fake article about the origins of individual intelligence (Hong et al., 1999). Although this fake article benefited its readers, Hong's research does not mean that we should mislead our students. Instead, we should translate her idea to the grade that we teach.

In this case, Hong wanted students to understand that a person's intelligence can change. Teachers have many ways to accomplish this mission.

- First graders might draw pictures of brains changing as they learn.
- Eighth graders might study neural network formation.
- High-school seniors might do research into axons, myelination, and neurotransmitters.

In a few sentences: **Don't obey. Don't imitate. Using your experience, *translate*.**

At times, MBE principle #2 feels liberating. A scientist's guidance, combined with our experience, opens up exciting new vistas of classroom possibility.

At other times, it feels frankly vexing. Our days are busy enough. We would just like someone to help us out and tell us exactly how to make a strategy work.

Alas, here's the stern truth: no one can do that but you. You are the only person teaching *these* students *this* curriculum in *this* school. And *only you are you*. A motivational phrase that fits your colleague just right might sound contrived or insincere coming from your mouth. Teachers aren't widgets. Research-based guidance needs to fit with our authentic teaching selves.

To remind you of this point, *Learning Grows* frequently suggests that you jot down your thoughts on translating a particular strategy. The more often you do so, the more helpful the book's guidance will be.

THIRD PRINCIPLE

For very good reasons, scientists almost always report averages. We look at average scores on quizzes or the average reaction time for particular stimuli or the average volume of a hippocampus.

Knowing these averages benefits teachers. For example, because retrieval practice helps students learn more *on average* than simple review, we can adopt this strategy in our own teaching.

At the same time, we must remember: averages apply to groups, not to specific people.

Here's MBE principle #3: **Averages matter, but no individual is average.**

This principle isn't a feel-good bromide to make everyone feel unicorn special. Instead, it articulates an important truth about psychology and humanity. Even if, for example, I have an average IQ, I almost certainly don't have average scores on all the subscales. And, even if I do, my visual working memory and my ability to inhibit extraneous thoughts and my empathy will certainly differ from the average (Rose, 2016).

For this reason, teachers should notice averages but always leave room for variety. After all, your class might average a 78 on a particular quiz. But you still want all your students—those who scored a 95 and those who scored a 44—to keep learning.

The motivation theories discussed here play nicely with all three principles. They offer teachers ways to think, not just instructions to follow (MBE #1). They leave room for teacherly translation. In fact, they frankly require teacherly translation (MBE #2). And, while they will help students near the middle of your "average," they provide healthy support for outliers as well (MBE #3).

The first book in this series—*Learning Begins*—focused on two topics: *working memory* and *attention*.

Working memory allows students—and the rest of us—to hold several ideas or processes in mind and put them together into some new combination. When you use phonics rules to sound out an unfamiliar word, you're using working memory. When you parse a word problem to calculate velocity or compare two pharaohs or take a new shortcut between two classroom buildings, you're holding and recombining information. That's all working memory (WM).

Alas, although students use WM all the time in school, they just don't have very much of it. For that reason, teachers need to be experts at working with our students' WM capacity. *Learning Begins* presents many (many) strategies to develop this expertise: how to *anticipate* WM overload and how to *identify* it when it happens. Of course, once we've anticipated and identified, we need strategies *to solve* WM problems as well.

Although relatively few teachers know about working memory, all of us know about attention. In particular, we know that students rarely pay enough of it. And yet, as explained in *Learning Begins*, a psychological approach to attention helps teachers view this problem in a whole new way.

Cognitive psychologists typically think of attention not as one thing but as a combination of three distinct mental processes: *alertness*, *orienting*, and *executive attention*. This framework helps us see that, although we can't solve attention problems directly, we can create attention by fostering its three subprocesses. *Learning Begins* devotes a chapter to each one, offering specific strategies to promote them all.

As you'll see, our understanding of motivation draws heavily on both these topics. In a sentence: demotivation (the topic of this book) interferes with learning primarily by muddling working memory and distracting attention (the topic of that book). We'll come back to both concepts frequently in *Learning Grows*. Chapter 6, in particular, reviews them in detail.

At times, the field of Mind, Brain, and Education feels like a lecture. Scientists tell teachers what to do. We listen, write it down, and then try to do it.

I hope that, instead, *Learning Grows* invites you to a conversation. Our teacherly expertise—combined with scientific perspectives and research paradigms—can generate fascinating and provocative ideas. Working collaboratively, teachers and psychologists and neuroscientists really can help our students learn.

That's why I wrote this book. That's why you're reading it.

Let's start talking.

Part I

MINDSET

Chapter One

Starting at the Fourth Step

Teachers often work with a basic learning flowchart in mind.

We start by introducing our students to a new topic or skill.

A biology teacher, for example, might launch the subject of Mendelian genetics. After some endearing stories of Monk Gregor pottering about in his pea patch, she introduces his ideas and explains their importance. She defines a few key terms ("phenotype," "allele") and breaks out the Punnett squares.

Students quickly get the hang of single-trait Punnett squares, and the class moves along to more intricate problems: say, dihybrid crosses.

Given the increasing complexity of these problems, her students probably don't solve them correctly at first. And yet, crucially, she sees no reason to worry. Our learning flowchart anticipates temporary struggle, even failure. If our students immediately succeeded at everything, we would most likely ramp up the difficulty of the curriculum.

After some trial and predictable error, this teacher's students get the hang of double heterozygotes. She can safely move on to meiosis.

In brief: after we introduce a topic, the students wrestle with it for a while. Once they've absorbed it well enough, we can all move on to the next topic.

The specifics for this flowchart look different if we're introducing spelling rules to first graders, photosynthesis to fourth graders, or the Declaration of Independence to eighth graders. But the model remains largely consistent, as depicted in figure 1.1.

It's important to emphasize that teachers should follow this educational model. We've got a groaning research library showing that *easy learning doesn't stick*. If students don't face occasional setbacks and generate mental sweat, then the ideas they understand today will fade with alarming speed. Robert Bjork and Elizabeth Ligon Bjork, and many others, have explored the benefits of "desirable difficulties": that is, the level of cognitive challenge

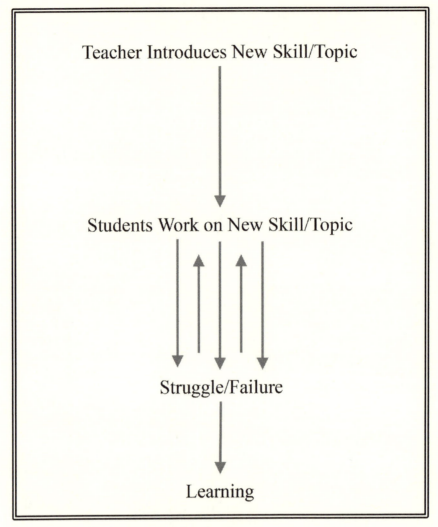

Figure 1.1. Basic Classroom Learning Flowchart

that yields enduring learning (Bjork & Bjork, 2014; Brown, Roediger, & McDaniel, 2014). (*Learning Thrives*, the next book in this series, will explore the benefits of desirable difficulties in loving detail.)

Because most work in school assumes regular cognitive struggle, and research shows that such struggles are beneficial, we teachers should ask ourselves: Do our students agree with us? Do they believe that cognitive struggle helps them learn?

For several decades now, we've known that many don't. In fact, most students fall—at least temporarily—into one of two groups.

CHARGE!

The first student group greets school challenges with energy and enthusiasm. Researchers have mapped this response in three clear ways: emotions, thoughts, and actions.

First, *emotionally*, these students respond with excitement and curiosity. They seem almost jazzed to have come across something they don't yet understand or can't yet do. They light right up with good cheer.

Second, *cognitively*, struggle helps these students sharpen their thought processes. When solving easy problems, they quickly figure out the basic strategies. When facing more vexing problems, however, they rise to a higher level of understanding. They find new, subtler approaches. They combine ideas in novel ways. They get better at whatever they're doing.

Third, *behaviorally*, these students willingly return to the scene of their setback. When the work gets harder, they smile, crinkle their brows, and redouble their efforts. They don't stop at upbeat emotions and effective thoughts. They get back to work.

Putting their emotions, cognitions, and behavior together, we see that they respond to difficulty by shouting, *"Charge!"*

RETREAT!

The second student group responds to struggle with a despondent, helpless sigh.

Emotionally, they feel embarrassed or angry or depressed. Their difficulties bring on a dour bout of gloom.

Cognitively, they take meaningful steps backward. The strategies that they had initially figured out while solving simple problems desert them. Far from making mental progress, they lose track of the ideas they had already understood.

Behaviorally, they give up. Unsurprisingly, given their emotional and cognitive collapse, they take the earliest opportunity to do something else.

Like King Arthur's knights in Monty Python's *Holy Grail*, they respond to failure by shouting, *"Run away!"*

THE MOTIVATION PARADOX

Here, then, we arrive at a paradox: the first of many we'll find as we study motivation. The learning paradigm that we typically follow—the paradigm that research shows we should use—*demotivates* many students, resulting in apathy, even gloom (Dweck, 2000).

So a more realistic model looks like figure 1.2.

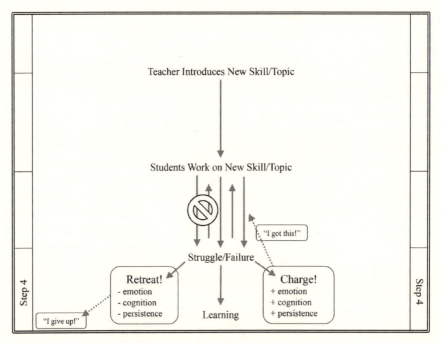

Figure 1.2. More Realistic Classroom Learning Flowchart

This learning flowchart reminds me of a student I'll call "Daniel." Daniel was assigned to my junior English class, and all I knew about him was that he would *never learn grammar*.

Let me explain.

To help our students write excellent essays, my English colleagues devoted substantial curricular time to teaching grammar. (Not all teachers agree that grammar helps with writing. If you don't, just bear with me.) To ensure that our students fully understood this material, sophomore year concluded with a substantial review test.

We prepared our students well, and so most passed, even though we set a passing grade at 75 percent. Those who didn't continued their grammar study during junior year.

As a junior English teacher, therefore, I needed to know how my incoming students had done. Although most had scored 75 percent or better, some were in the high 60s or low 70s. A few might have ended the year with a low 60 or—in the most extreme cases—a 58 or 59.

You can imagine my thoughts when I saw that Daniel scored a 44 percent.

I'd never even heard of a student with such a low score, much less taught one. What was I to do?

Immediately, Daniel's case raised questions of *motivation*. If grammar was so difficult for him, if he had been pounding his head against this wall all sophomore year and gotten only a 44 percent, what could possibly motivate him to start all over again? How could I ask that of him? He clearly was in full retreat; what might make him turn 180 degrees and charge?

This concern resonated with me especially because the subject was *grammar*. In my experience as an English teacher, some students just . . . well, they just don't do grammar. It's simply not their thing. They're often wonderful kids and able students. They participate in class discussion and complain amiably about vocabulary tests and have lots to say about *Romeo and Juliet*. But for some reason, grammar doesn't work for their brains. They haven't learned it; they don't learn it; they never will learn it.

(In my professional development work with teachers, I often see English teachers nodding their heads in resignation when I describe this grammar incapacity.)

And so, if Daniel simply couldn't learn grammar, how on earth could I motivate him to try?

My work with Daniel turned out to be an important pivot in my teaching career, and so I'll come back to his story in succeeding chapters. For the time being, keep in mind this motivational puzzle. Doubtless you've worked with a few Daniels of your own.

COUNTING DOWN FROM FOUR

As you might have noticed, figure 1.2 labels the charge vs. retreat moment as "step 4." This numbering system raises obvious questions and requires a brief explanation.

Question #1: *You left out steps 1 through 3. What happened to them?*

This question points to a key insight in motivation research: it's often hard to identify the correct starting point.

From the *teacher's* perspective, the moment of retreat feels like the place to start. When we see retreat behaviors—pointless complaining, refusal to participate, grouchy pouting—we might think: "Aha! I should focus here. I'll motivate them so that their behavior improves!"

From a *student's* perspective, however, retreat is less a cause and more a result. It results from several prior mental processes: processes that this book will eventually call "step 1," "step 2," and "step 3."

To solve this motivation problem, teachers shouldn't start with students' retreat behavior. We should instead start with all of those prior mental processes.

Sadly, those "prior mental processes" take place internally and invisibly. They're hard to spot, harder still to identify and diagnose. The research that we'll study in part I helps us solve this problem.

Question #2: *Okay, it makes sense that we need to start with internal mental processes, not the behavior itself. So bring it on: what is step 1?*

Have faith: we will get to step 1. However, the theory will make much more sense if we get there slowly. Psychology research started with step 4. In fact, it didn't get to step 1 until a few decades later. If we follow its historical development, the argument will be much easier to understand.

We should also postpone a discussion of step 1 because it can lead to tunnel vision. Our profession has spent a great deal of time focusing on step 1: so much time that we've ignored the others. As a result, we often oversimplify—even misunderstand—step 1, which makes sense only in light of steps 2 through 4.

This 4-3-2-1 organization attempts to rebalance our profession's understanding of the full theory. Rather than obsessing over just one portion of it, we need to see its full power and complexity. When we do, we can use the theory more effectively. To put that in other words: we'll be better at motivating our students.

SEARCHING FOR STEP 3

Given our alarm at figure 1.2, where many students simply opt out, teachers quickly focus on an essential goal. To help all our students learn, we want to convert our *retreat!* students into *charge!* students.

Let's note this important distinction: we don't exactly want to motivate students; we want them not to be *de*motivated. If more of our students gravitate to the right side of figure 1.2, then we don't need to wave pom-poms and gin up exaggerated enthusiasm. Students who find academic challenges intrinsically motivating have much less need of extrinsic motivators.

Psychologists offer us this guidance: we can help *retreaters* learn to *charge* only if we understand what made them retreat (and others charge) in the first place. We need to find step 3 and see why it leads to step 4.

False Start

As psychologists began exploring this question in the 1960s, they started with the most straightforward hypothesis. They posited that *capable* students respond to setbacks by shouting, *"Charge!"* while *weaker* students cry, *"Retreat!"*

You might say that students respond appropriately based on their skill level. Strong students—who will no doubt arrive at success after enough mental effort—keep working. Weaker students—who, alas, may never fully understand this material—are simply saving themselves time by giving up now.

For instance, a student who has always been good at math might suddenly find herself struggling to understand base eight. She has been writing the number "8" for years and might well wonder why she now is writing "10" after the number "7." At the same time, given her prior successes with math, she knows that she'll figure out this new system relatively quickly, and so she hastens back into the mental fray. She's as excited, thoughtful, and determined as ever.

This same student, however, has struggled with Latin for years. All those genders and all those case endings just seem too overwhelming to track. When facing a lesson explaining the use of the ablative—it can show both time and place, both location and separation—she quickly fires up her Instagram account. Hard experience has shown that she'll never understand this mystery, and she sees no reason to keep banging her forehead against Latin grammar. *Retreat!*

This "skill level" hypothesis has the strength of being easy to understand. It suffers the weakness of being wrong. Over and over, when we test this idea, we find that *ability does not predict step-4 response to struggle* (Dweck & Sorich, 1999; Mueller & Dweck, 1998). A student who has always felt at home with math's intricacies might curl up like a hedgehog when suddenly stumped by base eight. A student baffled by even simple Latin declensions might nonetheless seize her ablative exercises with evident cheer.

To solve the step-4 puzzle, we need to keep looking for an evidence-based step 3.

Firmer Footing

In the 1970s, two researchers—Carol Diener and Carol Dweck—pondered a new hypothesis about step 4 (S4). Diener and Dweck knew that students' skill level didn't account for differences between retreaters and chargers. They wondered if, instead, students' *response* to struggle at step 4 depended on their *explanations* for struggle at step 3 (S3).

Picture this scenario: in an art history class, Mary-Kate struggles with Impressionism. She gets a C- on a test that her classmates call "easy." Thinking over her difficulties, she explains them to herself by frankly acknowledging her own lapses.

Mary-Kate knows she could have done the reading more carefully before class. She could have taken better notes while the teacher was contrasting Manets and Monets. She admits that she checks her phone frequently while studying for tests. Put simply, she *explains* her difficulties by *accepting responsibility for her lack of effort*.

However, Mary-Kate's twin sister—let's call her Ashley—offers an alternative narrative to explain her own difficulties. Ashley tells herself that she simply doesn't have what it takes to learn about art. Some people have that ability; some don't. Ashley considers herself one of the "don'ts."

Of course, it can be embarrassing to admit this disability. For that reason, Ashley might be inclined to emphasize others' failures. She points out that the art history textbook is boring and confusing. She explains that a nearby student's cough sounded like a cat bringing up hairballs. She opines that the teacher created an utterly unreasonable test—one that Renoir himself could not have understood, much less passed. Unlike Mary-Kate, Ashley *explains* her academic difficulties by *blaming something else to disguise her perceived lack of ability*.

Diener and Dweck hypothesized that these different step-3 explanations for struggle would generate profoundly different motivational pathways.

By accepting responsibility for her lack of effort, Mary-Kate focuses on behaviors she can fix. During the subsequent Picasso and Matisse unit, she can read the chapter scrupulously. She can attend more carefully to the teacher's slides. She can turn her phone to airplane mode while studying. By making all these changes, she will no doubt learn a great deal about modernist masters. Because effort problems can typically be solved, acknowledging them motivates students to work harder.

That is, a student who *sees struggle as a symptom of insufficient effort* should be more likely to charge at S4.

On the other hand, Ashley's belief that she lacks ability—like her habit of assigning blame—means that she has little power to fix anything. She can't improve the textbook. She can't cure her classmate's cough. She can't change the teacher's test. Facing all these immutable problems, helpless Ashley might just as well give up.

That is, a student who *sees struggle as a symptom of insufficient ability* should be more likely to retreat at S4.

(To be clear: resemblance between these twin sisters and any famous twin sisters is entirely accidental.)

To test their hypothesis, Diener and Dweck gathered together 130 fifth graders for a multi-step experiment (Diener & Dweck, 1978). Because this study introduces so many key paradigms in motivation research, we're going to investigate its details. At the same time, it will be helpful to start off with the big picture.

The big picture: first, Diener and Dweck needed to find students who explain struggle the Mary-Kate way ("I didn't work effectively") and others who explain it the Ashley way ("I just lack ability"). To find these students, they used a standard psychology questionnaire. Next, they needed the students to experience cognitive setbacks. For this step, they had their fifth graders take on an unfamiliar logic puzzle. Finally, they wanted to see how students responded to their setback. Specifically, they hypothesized that Mary-Kates would charge, while Ashleys would retreat.

To sort Mary-Kates from Ashleys, Diener and Dweck used a well-established questionnaire. Three dozen questions forced students to choose between effort and ability as an explanation for failure. For example, one question asked,

> When you find it hard to work arithmetic or math problems at school, is it because
> A) you didn't study well enough before you tried them, or
> B) the teacher gave problems that were too hard. (Crandall, Katkovsky, & Crandall, 1965, p. 96)

In this case, answer A clearly focuses on the student's effort. Answer B blames the teacher and the math problem themselves; they are just "too hard." It also admits the limitations in the student's ability: surely the problems wouldn't be too hard for a student with greater skills.

Diener and Dweck then looked for Ashley students, whose explanations focused consistently on ability, and Mary-Kate students, whose explanations focused on effort. (Those who had one foot in each explanation didn't continue in the study.)

Having found a group of Mary-Kates and a group of Ashleys, the researchers now needed them to experience a school-like cognitive difficulty. They had the fifth graders try a mental exercise: a logic puzzle structured like a guessing game. Students looked at rows of shapes—like the ones in figure 1.3—and tried to deduce which shape the researcher had in mind. As you can see, each row has six possibilities: big triangle, big square, little star, little circle, or—to mix it up a bit—horizontal lines or vertical lines.

Figure 1.3. Logic Puzzle. *Adapted from "An Analysis of Learned Helplessness: Continuous Changes in Performance, Strategy, and Achievement Cognitions Following Failure," by C. I. Diener & C. S. Dweck, 1978, Journal of Personality and Social Psychology, 36(5), p. 453. Copyright 1978 by the American Psychological Association.*

If they guessed wrong on the first row, they could try again on the second and the third and so on until they ran out of rows.

But there was a catch. When the students announced their guess, they were instructed not to name the shape itself ("I guess circle") but to say which *side* of the diagram the shape was on ("It's on the right"). A student who believed that the researcher was thinking about the star would say "left" for the first row. For the second row, she would say "right."

If, on the other hand, the student guessed that the researcher was focused on the square, she would say "right, right, left, right."

This part of the study took place in three phases.

In Phase I, Diener and Dweck wanted these students to experience success. For that reason, both groups got several easy puzzles. These eight puzzles had many rows and provided feedback after every row, so all the students got them all correct. Both ability-conscious Ashleys and effort-conscious Mary-Kates must have been feeling good about their puzzle-solving skills.

In Phase II, Diener and Dweck wanted students to experience struggle, and so they made the puzzles dramatically harder. The students got feedback less frequently—after every fourth row—and had few rows to examine. As a result, by design, none of the students solved any Phase II puzzles. After their early successes, these fifth graders endured a string of obvious failures.

You can see that this exercise mirrors our classroom flowchart (figure 1.1). Like teachers everywhere, Diener and Dweck presented a new topic: a fun logic puzzle. They then gave students some straightforward practice problems to acclimate them to this new work: the easy Phase I puzzles. Once students got the hang of the new idea, the researchers ramped up the practice problem difficulty: the Phase II challenging puzzles.

Phase III explored the essential question: how did these challenging problems affect students' motivation at S4? After a period of struggle, did they rebound—like *charge!* students—or give up—like *retreat!* students?

As Diener and Dweck predicted, *effort-conscious students charged.*

In the first place, they deliberately engaged their cognitive gears. For example, they regularly coached themselves through the difficult problems, saying things like "I should slow down and try to figure this out" or "The harder it gets the harder I need to try." They remained emotionally upbeat; one effort-focused student commented, "I love a challenge," whereas another exhorted himself, "I've almost got it now" (Diener & Dweck, 1978, p. 459).

Just as important, these students got better at solving problems. In Diener and Dweck's phrasing, they became "more strategic."

Pretend that you're a fifth grader and look again at the first row of figure 1.3. If you believe the researcher is thinking of "triangle," you would guess "left." If the researcher says "incorrect," you've learned that she *isn't* thinking of the triangle.

But you've *also* learned that she isn't thinking of the other shapes on the left: "star" and "horizontal lines." With one word of feedback, you were able to eliminate three incorrect answers. And so, when you ask about the second row, you've only got three possible shapes left. This insight allows you to be "more strategic" and thereby sleuth your way toward the correct answer more deftly.

It was quite rare for students in either group to have this "strategic" insight during the first two phases. However, during Phase III, effort-focused students made this leap more than 30 percent of the time. Remarkably, experiencing cognitive setback helped them learn.

Overall, students who interpreted setback as a lack of effort maintained their emotional composure during struggle. And after struggle, they got better at the logic puzzles.

On the contrary, *ability-focused students sounded the retreat*. Rather than encouraging themselves during the difficulties of Phase II, they began dwelling on their deficits: "This isn't fun anymore," said one, while another lamented, "I never did have a good rememory." ("Rememory" is adorable, no?) Unlike the effort-focused students, their ability-focused peers started making comments irrelevant to the task: "There is a talent show this weekend, and I am going to be Shirley Temple," one winsomely announced (Diener & Dweck, 1978, pp. 458–59).

Whereas effort-focused students became more strategic after failure, those attuned to a lack of ability increasingly adopted useless strategies. In some cases, they always guessed "left" no matter what feedback they got. In others, they stuck with their choice even after being told that it was wrong. For instance, one ability-focused student kept guessing "star," explaining that he really liked constellations.

Overall, students who interpreted setback as a lack of ability consistently retreated. Their negative emotions took over, and their cognitive effectiveness sharply declined.

∼

To sum up: Diener and Dweck have found a persuasive answer to the S3 puzzle that stumped earlier psychologists. Students often give up when they believe that their struggles result from a lack of ability. After all, because they cannot magically get better, they feel no motivation to keep up the hard work. However, students who accept that difficulties result from a lack of effort have reason to gird their loins and redouble their toil. If they work more effectively, they know that they can overcome their difficulties and make real progress.

Starting at the Fourth Step

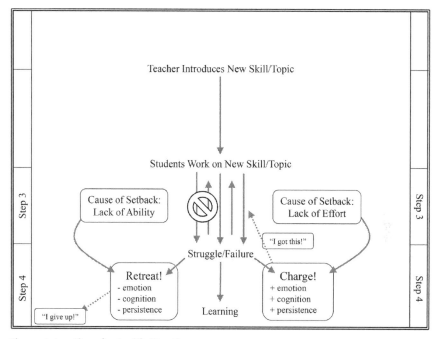

Figure 1.4. Flowchart with Step 3

In a sentence: if I tell you how a student *explains* setbacks, you can tell me how he *responds* to them. Step 3 leads directly to step 4 (figure 1.4).

CLASSROOM STRATEGIES AT STEP 3

Diener and Dweck's early insight gives us a straightforward motivational strategy: we should encourage students to rethink their explanations for struggle. When we help them focus on the mental sweat they generate rather than the level of ability they believe they have, we automatically prompt them to charge when they might have retreated. They used to hang out on the left side of figure 1.4, but they start getting more comfortable on the right side.

How then can we best help them refocus from cognitive talent to cognitive determination? What specific classroom strategies should teachers adopt?

Sadly, some teachers infer that this transition might be difficult, even impossible. Labels such as "effort-conscious student" imply that these identities don't change. A student's fixation on effort might be like her right-handedness: an unalterable part of her identity.

This interpretation, although alarmingly common, has Dweck all wrong. Researchers don't see "focus on ability" and "focus on effort" as *settled parts of our identity* but as *responses to particular conditions* (Dweck, 2006). Although in the classroom Ashley blames her teacher for her Impressionist struggles, on the soccer pitch she might have a different perspective. She freely admits that she should have practiced more diligently before Saturday's embarrassing soccer loss. Rather than blame her cleats or her coach, she blames her inadequate physical preparation.

True enough, many people lean one way more often than the other. Diener and Dweck's questionnaire helped them find students who habitually adopted one stance. But few of these students always offered the same explanation. Like our students, they fell somewhere along an explanation continuum. They do not live solely in one camp or the other.

This insight profoundly shapes the nature of our goal. To help ability-conscious students become effort-conscious students, we needn't script dramatic conversion narratives. Instead, we can find quiet, even subtle encouragements to coax them in the right direction.

How, then, to begin this coaxing? Dweck's best-known teaching suggestion came as quite a surprise indeed.

Sure-Footed Praise

Dweck's initial suggestion sounded distinctly like heresy.

During the 1970s and 1980s, American culture was very much in the grips of the "self-esteem movement." This theory argued that children develop best when they feel good about themselves, and therefore adults should do everything we can to help them glow with pride. Thus was born the participation trophy and all the other tchotchkes that reward children even when they haven't done anything to merit a reward.

This theory turned out to have the cause-and-effect relationship backward. We feel good about ourselves when we accomplish something of real value, but we don't necessarily accomplish things of real value just because we feel good about ourselves. Nonetheless, sadly, the emphasis on building self-esteem meant that children got used to regular praise and reassurance (Baumeister & Tierney, 2011).

Dweck, swimming against this cultural current, dared to wonder if all that praise had the opposite effect it intended. Specifically—working with Claudia Mueller—she hypothesized that praise might influence students' S3 explanations for their academic struggles. They envisioned two scenarios.

When my student offers a compelling insight during a discussion of genes or deftly analyzes the Treaty of Brest-Litovsk or correctly spells a complicated word, she merits a teacherly compliment.

- "Wow," I say, "Barbara McClintock would say that you're *really smart*. And I agree!"
- "Only a *gifted historian* would see how Brest-Litovsk served as a model for the Treaty of Versailles."
- "You see class: *intelligent students* remember that 'Wednesday' has a hidden 'd' and a hidden 'e'!"

By calling my student "smart," "gifted," and "intelligent," I obviously boost her self-esteem.

However, when my student notices that I highlight her mental *ability*, she learns to do so as well. At some inevitable future point when she doesn't succeed, she—like Ashley muddling the Impressionists—can conclude that she's reached the outer limits of her ability.

Her knack for science covers biology but not chemistry. She has the gift for WWI history but not for Egyptian pharaohs. She's intelligent enough to spell "Wednesday" but embarrassed when "caught" or "straight" or "disappear" reveals the limits of her spelling bee intelligence.

My compliments for intelligence highlight her ability, and as Diener and Dweck have shown, students focused on ability often *retreat*.

On the other hand, Mueller and Dweck imagined another kind of compliment, one that focuses on the student's *effort*.

- "Wow," I might say, "Barbara McClintock *worked for years* to come up with that theory. It looks like you *put in a lot of time* to understand it, too. Well done!"
- "Did you *make a grid* comparing Brest-Litovsk's main points with those of Versailles? It clearly helped you see deep connections."
- "I saw that your flashcards *highlighted* the hidden 'd' and 'e' in 'Wednesday.' Your *extra preparation* paid off."

Because these compliments point to the work my student did, they encourage him to value such work. When he—like Mary-Kate squinting at a Renoir—faces a classroom setback, he'll probably conclude he needs to apply some mental elbow grease. If he's going to understand stoichiometry or Pharaoh Akhenaten's reign or the secret to spelling "stretch," he knows that mental effort will get him there.

In this case, my compliments for a student's work highlight his effort, and as Diener and Dweck have shown, focus on effort prompts students to *charge*.

Praising Smarter, Praising Harder

To test this compliment hypothesis, Mueller and Dweck conducted a series of six experiments, working again with fifth graders and logic puzzles (1998).

The big picture: Mueller and Dweck gave students a logic puzzle—not the shape puzzle we saw above—and praised them in different ways for their reported success. When the students tried a second round of those puzzles, their reported scores fell dramatically. Mueller and Dweck hypothesized that the students' response to this setback would vary depending on the praise they heard. They measured this result in many ways. You will recognize several of these measurements, although a few offer fresh kinds of insight. The final one is really a shocker.

In the first study, students met with researchers individually. They were given simple logic puzzles to solve and were then praised for their success. (Mueller and Dweck pretended that everyone had gotten the same score, no matter what their actual score had been.)

- One-third of the students—the control group—were praised for getting 80 percent correct: "Wow, you did very well on these problems. That's a really high score."
- One-third of the students heard an extra ability-focused sentence: "Wow, you did very well on these problems. That's a really high score. You must *be smart* at these problems."
- The final third, instead, heard an extra effort-focused sentence: "Wow, you did very well on these problems. That's a really high score. You must have *worked hard* at these problems" (Mueller & Dweck, 1998, p. 36, emphasis added).

The students then did another group of puzzles, this one noticeably harder than the first. As a result, Mueller and Dweck reported that their scores fell to 50 percent. (Again, it didn't matter what their real scores were. By the way, they chose this puzzle because fifth graders couldn't really be sure how well they had done and so wouldn't be suspicious about these lower scores.)

The researchers wondered how students would respond to struggle at S4 after receiving compliments that shaped S3. Specifically, they wondered if this slightly different praise—you must "be smart" vs. you must have "worked hard"—would cause retreating or advancing.

Starting at the Fourth Step 19

This hypothesis seems quite a stretch. After all, for these fifth graders, only two or three words differed over an hour. It seems hard to imagine that such a small change could produce any meaningful results. And yet, this seemingly inconsequential change had consequences.

As before, researchers had many ways to measure students' responses.

First, they looked at students' explanations for their lower score. Students who heard that they "must be smart" blamed their struggles on a lack of ability twice as often as they blamed lack of effort. Students who heard that they "must have worked hard" reversed that result. They were twice as likely to focus on effort to explain their lower score.

As predicted, a compliment after success can shape an S3 understanding of mistakes.

According to Diener and Dweck's earlier research (1978), these different explanations for difficulty should have led some students to retreat and others to charge. Did they?

To analyze this question, Mueller and Dweck returned to familiar categories: students' emotions, their thoughts, and their behaviors.

Emotions: students rated their enjoyment of the logic puzzles on a one-to-six scale. Those praised for "being smart" rated their enjoyment just over a 4, whereas those praised for "working hard" rated their enjoyment just under a 5.

A difference of less than one point might not seem like much. If you study statistics, however, you'll be impressed to know that the p-value was less than 0.001 and that Cohen's d was 0.90. (If you don't study stats, take note: such numbers would get Nate Silver's attention.)

More persuasively, perhaps, recall that Mueller and Dweck caused this change by *swapping two-word phrases*: "be smart" and "worked hard." If a mere two words can move students from "I slightly enjoyed these puzzles" to "I mostly enjoyed these puzzles," those words deserve our respect.

Thoughts: Mueller and Dweck—like Diener and Dweck before them—found that effort-focused students became "more strategic." In one of their six experiments, both student groups solved, on average, roughly 4.70 problems during the first round. Students praised for effort ultimately improved their performance by 26 percent. Those praised for ability saw an alarming drop off: -4 percent.

As Mueller and Dweck note, this second result especially merits our attention. Students should be getting better at these logic puzzles simply because they've had the chance to *practice*. Those in the control group, who got neither compliment, saw average scores rise 8 percent. And yet, this practice didn't benefit students praised for being smart. Once they faced a setback, they retreated; their scores fell, practice or no practice.

Behaviors: these fifth graders also rated the likelihood that they would want to continue doing these puzzles at home. Students praised for ability hedged their bets; on average, they said "possibly." Student praised for effort jumped on board. They said "probably" or "very probably." Again, very slight changes in language produced an impressively large difference in behavior.

Mueller and Dweck used another approach to measure students' behavioral responses. Students were given the chance to look at one of two folders. The first one contained "problem-solving strategies." Of course, anyone wanting to improve—that is, to charge—would pick this folder. The second folder contained other students' scores on the logic puzzle. This folder wouldn't help a student improve—but it would let him know where his ability ranked compared to peers.

No doubt you can anticipate their findings. Fourteen percent of students praised for their gifts looked at "problem-solving strategies." This result makes a grim kind of sense: who needs strategies if you're gifted? By contrast, 77 percent of students praised for their work pored over those strategies. A student determined to work hard, no doubt, will be glad for an expert's guidance.

One final, quite astounding result stands out from this collection of experiments. Mueller and Dweck suspected that people who focus primarily on intelligence will do many things to display it, including *lie*.

To test this glum idea, they gave students a chance to mislead their peers. Students wrote up anonymous descriptions of their experience for classmates to read. Mueller and Dweck wanted to know if students would report their scores honestly.

In the control group, 14 percent of the students exaggerated their scores. In the effort-praise group, 13 percent exaggerated their scores. Clearly, praise that emphasized "hard work" did not encourage dishonesty.

And yet—spooky music please—of the students praised for "intelligence," fully 38 percent reported their test score dishonestly. Remarkably, telling a student that he must "be smart" nearly *triples* the likelihood that he will lie about his grade. When teachers imply that intelligence is the most important thing, students do what they need to do to demonstrate that intelligence . . . including conjuring falsehoods.

In sum: Just as Mueller and Dweck had hypothesized, small changes in language produced starkly different motivations. S3 *intelligence* compliments focused students on their *ability* and so caused them to *retreat* at S4—emotionally, cognitively, and behaviorally. On the other hand, S3 *effort* compliments focused students on their *work* and so promoted emotional, cognitive, and behavioral *engagement* at S4.

Classroom Translations

This study and others like it (e.g., Cimpian, Arce, Markman, & Dweck, 2007) suggest Dweck's best-known strategy for encouraging students to charge: praise the *process*, not the *person*. In other words, approve of the work the student did, not the person the student is.

The best way to enact this strategy will depend on the specifics of your teaching world. Your school's culture, your students' maturity, your class's curriculum, and your own personality will substantially shape the language that works best. To be meaningful, after all, compliments must sound sincere—and a compliment that comes from a script won't sound like the real you.

Two guidelines may help you find the phrasing that fits you best. First, you may know Doug Lemov's book *Teach Like a Champion, 2.0* (2015). In it, Lemov advocates the use of "precise praise." When we make our plaudits specific, when we name the details that made a student's work successful and good, we are automatically describing a process.

- Rather than saying, "This essay is excellent; you're clearly a natural!" try "This essay is excellent; your strategy of comparing Joseph Asagai to Jim O'Connor brought out surprising new ideas!"
- Rather than saying, "You're a very good girl," try "When you went straight to the carpet and stayed focused during silent reading, you showed your classmates the best way to learn."
- Rather than saying, "Only a genius could have done this," try "I saw you had to work this proof many times before you figured out such an elegant solution."

In each of these cases, you've replaced a compliment that emphasizes being a particular kind of person ("a natural," "a good girl," "a genius") with one that emphasizes doing a particular kind of work (comparing two characters, concentrating on a book, trying multiple solutions).

A recent analysis adds an important caveat to this kind of praise. Amemiya and Wang (2018) note that, especially in high school, students hear pure effort praise as a kind of consolation prize. They might infer a note of pity in an effort compliment: "You didn't get the answer right," teachers seem to say, "but at least you tried. That's better than nothing."

This helpful warning should encourage us to focus not simply on our students' mere *efforts* but also on their *strategies*. We can imagine three different versions of the same compliment:

1. (Ability praise) Your outline for your research project is great. You must get your gifts in historical research from your dad—it's in your heritage!
2. (Effort praise) Your outline for your research project is great. You must have put a lot of thought into it.
3. (Precise strategy praise) Your outline for your research project is great. Most people organize their projects chronologically. Your decision to organize by the political affiliation of the source will lead to surprising and helpful results.

The ability praise, alas, emphasizes the student's "gifts"—in fact, her *inherited* gifts. The effort praise, instead, highlights the student's thoughtfulness, not her natural gifts. The strategy praise—better still—moves beyond the mere amount of work to the qualities that make the work worthwhile. Especially when working with middle- and high-school students, we should translate as much praise as possible to this third version.

Doubtless it will take time to adapt to this new approach. You may find yourself slipping back into old, counterproductive habits. Dweck won't scold you if you do: "I am not saying that intelligence praise is the worst thing you can do to a child. Heaven knows there are many worse things, but as this work shows there are also clearly better things" (Dweck, 2000, p. 120).

One example in my own work stands out as especially humbling. During a presentation on motivation for a K–8 faculty, I put up a slide with a lengthy quotation. When I asked for someone to read it out loud, a teacher promptly volunteered, reading with rare grace and thoughtfulness. She spoke slowly enough for complex ideas to sink in but not so slowly as to bore her colleagues. She used punctuation to make sense of the more intricate sentences, giving each comma its due. She quickly saw a bit of levity in the passage and emphasized just the right words to punch up the humor.

Delighted by her reading, I cried out: "Brava! You were brilliant!"

Immediately, I recognized a dreadful irony. While summarizing Dweck's guidance, I had contradicted Dweck's guidance. Even as I advocated precise praise for good work ("You emphasized the subtle humor in that passage very effectively"), I slipped back into old routines and praised the person ("You're brilliant!").

My mistake highlights an important point: changing teacherly habits takes focus, patience, and occasional self-forgiveness. If you've been complimenting your "gifted" students for years, you will almost certainly find yourself doing so again. Rather than put yourself down for such lapses, use them as opportunities to practice this new skill. Ask yourself: what did the student just *do* to earn the compliment "gifted"? Then rephrase your compliment with that new focus. The exchange might sound like this: "Wow! This is gifted work! [brief pause] And by that I mean you used the word 'jogging' as both a gerund and a participle. This flexibility shows deep understanding of the material."

A second guideline might also help you improve your compliments. Especially if you want to practice your understanding of grammar, you might focus on parts of speech. Typically, when we praise with *nouns and adjectives*, we are slipping into the world of person praise:

- "You are obviously *gifted*!"
- "You're clearly *a natural* when it comes to history research."
- "Only a *born dancer* could have executed that pirouette."

If, instead, we switch to *verbs and adverbs*, we will almost certainly turn our focus to students' actions:

- "You *repeatedly revised* this draft, and that work shows in the final result."
- "You *showed* all your work, and as a result you *caught* your mistake on the third step here: well done."
- "Both of you clearly *rehearsed* this scene several times outside of class, and that extra effort really paid off in the pacing."

While this part-of-speech guideline isn't absolute, you might find it a helpful shorthand when conjuring compliments for your students.

As a test case, consider the word "organized." Is calling a student "organized" person praise or process praise? Take a moment to see if you can make arguments on both sides of that question.

On the one hand, the compliment "organized" fails both guidelines above. Contra Lemov, it isn't terribly precise. And, contra the part-of-speech test, it's an adjective. (More precisely, it's a participle: an adjective that started life as a verb.) For these reasons, you might hesitate to call a student "organized."

On the other hand, the word "organized" naturally emphasizes work that the student is doing—in this case, she's *organizing*. While it's clear that not everyone can be a genius, it's just as clear that everyone can be organized: organizing is an action that anyone can do. For this reason, "organized" feels more like process praise than person praise.

Of course, it would be improved by giving it Lemovian precision: "Your lab report is very well organized. When you used colors for different lines on your graph, you made it especially easy to sort through the variables. Well done."

To solidify this teaching strategy, you might try two steps. First, take five minutes right now and think about the compliments that you use most often in your teaching. You might even list them. Once you've gotten them down on paper, ask yourself: am I showing admiration for the work my students do or for the kind of people they are?

Second, understand that you might find this listing task surprisingly difficult. Our praise phrases come so naturally to us that we might not even be aware of them. For this reason, you might ask a colleague to visit your class simply to keep track of the praise language that you use. A wise and sympathetic ear—especially one attached to a head that understands this research—can provide real insight to you and real benefit to your students.

If you've had good luck with technology, you might also try recording your classes. When you review the tapes, you can listen for the praise phrases that appear most often.

Criticism: Ours and Theirs

The following story is true. The names have been changed to protect my very innocent mother.

Once upon a time, there was a young girl trying to learn Latin. The grammar system didn't come easily to her, and so she struggled with the in-class exercises. This young girl's teacher—let us call him Mr. Badman—would stand in front of her and pound on her desk, crying: "How can you be so STUPID?! How can you be SO STUPID?!"

The young girl grew up to be a splendid human being (and a wonderful mother). She did not, however, end up learning much Latin.

When teachers hear that Dweck has advice about criticism, we might initially assume that she will warn us away from the Badman Method. Doubtless research can show that calling students "so stupid" demotivates them. (It is, after all, criticism about the kind of person they are, not the kind of work they did.) Research might also show that it's really mean.

Here again, researchers have explored counterintuitive ideas. They worry less about Mr. Badman, and more about teachers who are altogether *too nice* when giving feedback. Paradoxically, the very kindness that prompted us to be teachers in the first place might lead us to critique our students counterproductively.

For example, Eddie Brummelman's research team wondered how adults might respond to children with low self-esteem (Brummelman et al., 2014). They found a troubling pattern. Adults tended to give low-self-esteem children *person* praise: "You are a *good drawer*." They gave high-self-esteem children *process* praise: "You *did a good job drawing*" (Brummelman et al., 2014, p. 10). In other words: the children most at risk for demotivation got the demotivating praise.

At first, it seems deeply implausible that this minor change in wording would make any difference. As one researcher notes, these compliments are "so similar, in fact, that adults may not be aware of their contrasting implications and are thus likely to use them interchangeably" (Cimpian et al., 2007, p. 314). And yet, as we have seen, even very small changes in wording shape children's thoughts. Subtle shifts in emphasis from smarts to grit can help children solve more puzzles and even tell fewer lies.

In fact, these very compliments—"you did a good job drawing" and "you are a good drawer"—have been studied by Cimpian et al. (2007). Very consistently, specific praise for work ("good job drawing") helped kindergartners charge, whereas generic ability praise ("good drawer") prompted them to retreat.

Other researchers (Rattan, Good, & Dweck, 2012) explored similar questions when they surveyed college students and teaching assistants (TAs). When TAs thought about guidance for a student who had failed a recent test, they supported the idea of assigning him less homework. They brought up the subject of dropping the class. They even suggested telling him that "not everyone is meant to pursue a career in this field" or "not everyone has math talent—some people are 'math people' and some people aren't" (Rattan et al., 2012, pp. 733–34).

You might respond to this finding with skepticism. Certainly I did. I simply couldn't imagine myself saying to a student, "Don't worry if you're no good at understanding poetry. I bet you're unusually good in your ethics class."

And yet, in recent years, I've seen firsthand evidence that teachers really might say such things. Specifically, since I began writing this book, several Facebook friends have posted a "letter from a principal in Singapore." You may have seen this letter, too.

This letter clearly comes from a kind person. The principal, noting that statewide exams will soon begin, encourages parents not to overemphasize mere test scores: "If your child doesn't [get top marks] . . . please don't take away their self-confidence and dignity from them. Tell them it's OK, it's just an exam! They are cut out for much bigger things in life." In an age obsessed with standardized test scores, this principal keeps a humane focus on long-term healthy development.

And yet, the letter also includes this remarkable passage:

> But, please do remember, amongst the students who will be sitting for the exams there is an artist, who doesn't need to understand Math. . . . There is an

entrepreneur, who doesn't care about History or English literature. . . . There is a musician, whose Chemistry marks won't matter. . . . There's an athlete . . . whose physical fitness is more important than Physics. (Dear Parents, 2017; ellipses in the original)

These statements seem preposterous. Does anyone really believe that "artists don't need math"? Or that businessmen don't need the moral guidance offered by history and literature?

And yet, the "principal's" advice surely comes from kindness. He or she wants to keep students' stress levels manageable and to focus on the long-term meaning of their education. In pursuit of these admirable goals, however, that guidance has gone dramatically astray.

I should note, by the way, that I'm skeptical this letter really comes from "a principal in Singapore." Extensive Internet searching yields little support for that claim—other than a photograph of a letter that doesn't seem to be on letterhead. The "principal" prefers strikingly informal grammar and punctuation: ten ellipses in three brief paragraphs. (I'm told that, in Singapore, this letter circulates under the heading "Letter from an American Principal.")

What matters here is not that a principal really wrote the letter but that eight or ten of my Facebook friends clearly endorse its message. (Eight or ten might not sound like a lot, but I have only eight or ten Facebook friends; as a matter of percentage, those numbers are compelling.) Clearly, despite my initial skepticism, teachers really do think it's okay to tell students "don't worry that your French accent is so bad; I hear you're tops in your biology section."

What happens to our students when teachers do so?

To answer this question, Rattan asked college students to imagine this scenario: on the very first calculus test of the year, they score a 65 percent. The professor notices their disappointment and assures them that he really cares about their progress.

The professor continues with "comforting feedback."

- He tells them not to feel bad because "not everyone can be a 'math person.'"
- He promises not to call on them in class, in order that they not be embarrassed.
- He plans to give them easier homework.

Certainly this "comforting" feedback sounds like a kind approach. By offering understanding and reassurance, promising not to embarrass students in front of their calculus classmates, and assigning less-demanding homework, this professor has rejected the Mr. Badman approach. All this kindness might well motivate students to work harder in class.

And yet, that's not what happened. Students who read the "more comforting feedback" quickly inferred that the professor had focused on their mathematical *ability* and didn't think much of it. As in previous research, students who focused on ability at S3 retreated at S4; they rated their motivation in the class as below average. Notably, these deleterious results sprang not from a Mr. Badman-like cruelty but from an excess of professional caring.

Rattan's team tried an alternate approach with students who got "more strategic" feedback. The professor tells these students:

- They should start working with a tutor.
- He plans to call on them more often to see how well they are progressing.
- He will give them more challenging math tasks to practice difficult concepts.

This "strategic" feedback sounds like stern stuff indeed. By demanding they do extra work, calling on struggling students more often, and ramping up the homework difficulty, the professor might well embarrass and demotivate his students.

That's not how they reacted. Instead, they inferred that the professor had focused on their *effort* and believed that they could and should do more. As we've seen over and over, an emphasis on work at S3 encourages students to charge at S4. In this case, they rated their motivation in class as well above average.

The appropriate language for this encouragement will depend—of course—on our own teaching contexts. Second graders, sixth graders, and twelfth graders need different levels of classroom challenge. Some students—you know who they are—need a sterner gaze to drive home the message. Rather than promising "more challenging" problems, you might say you've got a special folder of puzzles for students who like to think about problems their own way.

Rattan's study, in other words, does not offer you a script to memorize. As MBE principle #2 tells us, we should not imitate but translate. Seen this way, Rattan's study offers a way to think about feedback for students who haven't yet learned the material. When we notice in ourselves a desire to "comfort" these students, we should ensure that our comforting words do not imply their inability. Instead, our kindness can prompt students to focus on continued mental exertion. Their motivation and learning will flourish.

"I Just Can't"

Up to this point, our discussion has focused on the teacher's feedback. Of course, students often comment on their own work. In fact, they can be their own harshest critics. If you've been teaching for any length of time, you have doubtless had a student tell you—with a plaintive voice and a downcast eye—"I just can't do it!"

Wanting to prompt such a student to charge at S4, I might be tempted to respond: "I'm sure you *can* do it." This response offers the right spirit of optimism. However, it includes two important drawbacks.

First, it's not true. At this very moment, the student in fact can't do it. He knows it, and I know it, and denying that obvious truth doesn't boost my credibility or enhance the student's learning.

Second, it might well feel insensitive, even dismissive. My student has just opened up about his failure and frustration to me, and I responded by telling him he's wrong.

Rather than rebuff him so directly, I would like to acknowledge his current difficulty frankly and also persuasively envision a more successful future. I want a magic word: one that allows me to empathize with his desire to retreat but gives him plenty of reason to charge.

That magic word exists. It is the word "yet."

When my student laments, "I just can't do it!" I take out my magic word and say "Well, you can't do it *yet*." With this response, I both acknowledge his present reality—a vexing feeling of failure—and promise a better future—a hopeful possibility of success.

- When your third grader announces, "Why are we doing this? I'll never understand multiplication with arrays!" you can say, "It's true that you don't understand arrays yet. But the reason we're practicing is so that you will."
- When a seventh grader bemoans his struggles with an assignment on Native American culture, saying that he "just doesn't get this stuff," don't say, "I'm sure you really do get it." Instead, respond that "it's okay if you don't get it yet. The role-play we'll be doing in today's class will help. Everyone makes progress at his own pace."
- When your leading lady announces, "I can't memorize this whole monologue," you might have responded, "I gotta say: last year's lead memorized all *her* lines." Now you can say, "You haven't memorized the speech yet. But you've been going over lines every night at home, and that work is paying off. Keep at it."

In each of these cases, the magical adverb "yet" looks to a more successful future without denying the troubled present.

I know of at least one school—Laurel School in the suburbs of Cleveland, Ohio—where teachers have adopted "yet" as an informal academic slogan. Many of them wear buttons emblazoned with this magic word.

Even *Sesame Street* has gotten on board with this magic word. In 2014, they made a video with Janelle Monáe singing about "The Power of Yet" while various Muppets can't—and then can—sing songs, play drums, add numbers, and write tricky letters (www.youtube.com/watch?v=XLeUvZvuvAs).

Starting at the Fourth Step   29

This video does have a quirky gap in it: only rarely does Monáe tell a struggling Muppet that "you can't do it . . . yet." The crucial verbal formulation, the one that discourages retreating and encourages charging, gets lost in the busy lyrics and dance steps.

This lapse might cause *Sesame Street* producers to want to retreat and stop airing the song. Although they haven't gotten the song exactly right *yet*, I hope they charge. They can, after all, revise the lyrics, reshoot the video, and improve their work.

In summary: Our responses to students' work shapes S3 and thereby nudges them to charge at S4.

When they succeed, we should ensure that our praise highlights their strategic efforts, not their IQs. When they struggle, we should beware the direction that our kindness might lead us. Finally, when they criticize themselves by insisting that "they just can't do it," the simple word "yet" can refocus them on the importance of continued strategic practice.

Figure 1.5 sums up this chapter's strategies.

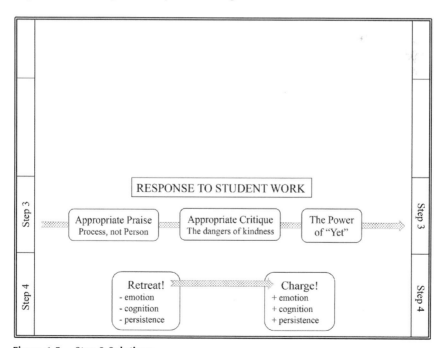

Figure 1.5.   Step 3 Solutions

So far, we have explored why students retreat or charge *after they've already begun their work*. We've looked at strategies to help them charge *once they've succeeded or struggled*. Chapter 2 asks this provocative question: can we predict their motivation even *before they begin working*? Can we encourage them to charge *even before they pick up a pencil*?

Chapter Two

Second Step
Rehearsing, Not Performing

Chapter 1 began by announcing a problem. We know that effortless learning doesn't stick—that some degree of confusion and setback enhances long-term learning. And yet, in the 1960s, researchers found that confusion and setback consistently demotivate some students.

Happily, in the 1970s, Diener and Dweck found a partial explanation—and practical solutions—to that problem. If we help students understand their own struggles the right way at S3, this understanding itself creates the motivation to re-engage at S4. When students believe that they failed because they didn't put in the right kind of strategic effort, they naturally enough start doing so.

This budding theory has lots of research support and offers specific classroom strategies we can easily make our own.

At the same time, because it helps only *after* academic struggle and failure begin, it feels incomplete. Why wait? Most of us would like to intervene as early as possible in our students' thought processes. The flow chart at the beginning of chapter 1 shows that a great deal of learning takes place *before students begin their practice*. What might we do at that earlier point to help students find intrinsic motivation?

IN SEARCH OF STEP 2

In the 1980s, Dweck continued her efforts to understand the differences between students who charge and those who retreat at S4. Working with Elaine Elliott, she refocused on earlier stages of the learning process: step 2. Whereas *Diener* and Dweck considered students' explanations *after* they started struggling, *Elliott* and Dweck wondered if these students differed even *before* they sat down to work.

Specifically, Elliott and Dweck (1988) investigated the *goals* that students espoused before they began their schoolwork.

They hypothesized that some students attend school to demonstrate *how much they already know*. In Elliott and Dweck's language, they embrace "performance goals." For these students, class provides a stage where they can strut their cognitive stuff.

This performance goal motivates students in very specific ways. For example, if a colleague asks you, "What is 5×7?" you're likely to answer "35" quite promptly. Questions such as these require no thought and certainly no work.

Students with performance goals recognize that people who know things don't have to work at them. For this reason, they want not to be seen working. They strive for "effortless perfection" (Dweck, 2006, p. 41). Perversely, that is, performance goals discourage students from working. If they have to work in school—and certainly if they get *caught* working—then their performance of comprehensive knowledge just won't be very persuasive.

As Dweck summarizes this thought process: "Effort is a bad thing. It, like failure, means you're not smart or talented. If you were, you wouldn't need effort" (Dweck, 2006, p. 16).

Likewise, these students fear mistakes. Just as you didn't make a mistake when multiplying 5×7 because you know the answer, they too must not make any mistakes lest they reveal their own incomplete knowledge. To demonstrate their *flawless performance*, they focus keenly on points. Anything short of a *high test score* would unmask their performance. Like the Wizard of Oz, they would be revealed as a weak and fumbling man behind a tasseled, lime-green curtain.

On the other hand, Elliott and Dweck believed, students might attend school with different goals: say, to *learn more than they already know*. Rather than show off their current knowledge store ("performance goals"), they would instead strive to add to it. For students with these "learning goals," school helps make a good brain better.

Like performance goals, learning goals create distinct motivational pathways. Learning obviously requires work. When students first learned to swim or play Minecraft or perform magic tricks, they had to sweat. Any student hoping to learn something else, therefore, very much expects to put in lots of mental effort. Whereas performance goals discourage work, learning goals encourage students to roll up their cognitive sleeves.

Equally important, learning goals help students reinterpret mistakes. When pursuing performance goals, a student shuns all errors. A student who hopes to learn, on the other hand, finds them pertinent and useful.

If I do twenty homework problems and get fourteen of them correct, I am—of course—glad to see that I understand a substantial chunk of this new material. I'm also glad that my six mistakes reveal the part that I don't yet know. I can now look for patterns in my mistakes and focus quite narrowly on the weaknesses that hamper my understanding. Mistakes serve as helpful signposts, pointing to the most useful focus for my cognitive effort (Dweck & Leggett, 1988).

For example, a friend recently decided to take up chess in a semi-serious way. Being in her fifties, she thought this mental yoga might keep her cerebral cortex limber. She spends at least ten or fifteen minutes a day solving online chess puzzles.

Fairly early on my friend noticed that she routinely missed a sneaky chess move called a "smothered mate." (You force your opponent to block in her own king and then check it with an unassailable knight.) Because her repeated mistakes pointed so clearly to this tactic, she knew to look for smothered-mate opportunities more carefully. She has now become quite skillful at smothering—a gruesome but potent chess accomplishment.

Of course, all the chess puzzles she solved correctly felt good. But she learned more from the smothered-mate puzzles she got wrong.

As we've seen, performance goals push students to focus on high test scores. Learning goals, by contrast, push students to focus on progress. As long as they're getting better, they're achieving their goal.

For example: I know a highly competitive tennis player who frequently joins local ladders. When we met for lunch after a recent match, he regaled me with his great triumph that very morning. He lost the first set 6–4, won the second set 6–3, and then—in a dramatic third-set tie-breaker—lost 9–7.

For a tennis player pursuing performance goals, that story offers no triumph. This guy *lost*. What's he so excited about?

For a tennis player pursuing learning goals, however, the best part is yet to come. My friend had battled his opponent many times before and hadn't yet even taken a set from the guy, much less come close to winning it all. This ever-so-near-to-victory defeat clearly showed how much progress he had made. Because he focused not on his score but on his learning, he was able to see this match for what it was: an impressive success.

Figure 2.1 summarizes these additions to our model.

In Elliott and Dweck's hypothesis, performance goals and learning goals at S2 should help explain our central mystery: students' response to struggle at S4.

To test their hypothesis, Elliott and Dweck worked with yet another group of fifth graders, using the same logic puzzle about guessing shapes. They told half these students that the puzzle could "be a big help in school, because it

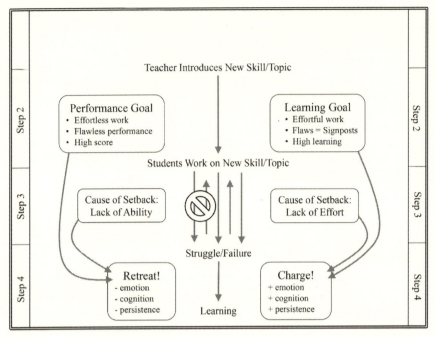

Figure 2.1. Flowchart with Step 2

'sharpens the mind' and learning to do it well could help their studies." These instructions clearly highlighted fifth graders' learning goals (LGs).

The other half, however, were told that they would be videotaped while they undertook the task and—just as daunting—graded on their performance by experts. With this set of instructions, Elliott and Dweck encouraged students to focus on "displaying competence"; in other words, to adopt performance goals (PGs) (Elliott & Dweck, 1988, p. 7).

To measure the effect of PGs and LGs, Elliott and Dweck kept track of three variables: the *choices* students made, the *strategies* they adopted, and the *words* they spoke.

Student choices: After they had been prompted to adopt either PGs or LGs, the students got to choose between two puzzles. One was described this way: "If you pick this box, although you won't learn new things, it will really show me what kids can do."

The second box came with this description: "If you pick the task in this box, you'll probably learn a lot of new things. But you'll probably make a bunch of mistakes, get a little confused, maybe feel a little dumb at times—but, eventually you'll learn some useful things" (Elliott & Dweck, 1988, p. 7).

As teachers, of course, we want our students to choose box #2. Our pedagogy expects that our students will "make a bunch of mistakes, get a little confused, maybe feel a little dumb at times." We know that temporary mental muddle will help them "learn some useful things."

Students prompted to adopt learning goals made exactly that choice. In fact, 84 percent of them chose box #2. Basically, six out of seven students with LGs chose a task that would help them learn—even though it included an explicit warning that they might feel "confused" and even "dumb." (By the way, it's incredibly rare for researchers to use words like "dumb" with students. Clearly, Elliott and Dweck wanted to offer a stark choice: to "learn useful things" sometimes requires feeling "dumb.")

In a dramatic contrast, only 34 percent of the performance-goal students chose box #2. Feeling motivated to show off their knowledge to the expert evaluator, they shied away from making "a bunch of mistakes" and instead wanted the chance to "really show what kids can do."

Because both boxes contained the same guess-what-I'm-thinking puzzle, Elliott and Dweck could compare the *strategies* that both groups used and the *emotions* they felt while working on them.

Student strategies: As we saw in chapter 1, this logic puzzle allows us to analyze the students' level of strategic thinking. When a savvy fifth grader heard that "left" was an incorrect answer, she could eliminate three possible guesses—not just the one she was asking about in the first place. Charging students often advanced to this analytical level.

On the other hand, less savvy fifth graders got caught up in foolish strategies: for example, always choosing "star" because they like the Big Dipper. Retreating students were especially prone to this kind of mistake.

Sure enough, Elliott and Dweck saw this same pattern. Students with learning goals at S2 were more likely to advance to savvy strategies at S4. Students with performance goals, however, were quicker to fall back to foolish "Big Dipper" strategies. Clearly, LGs promote cognitive acuity, whereas PGs interfere with it.

Student statements: As before, Elliott and Dweck asked these students to say what they were thinking; these statements fell into familiar patterns.

Fifth graders with PGs focused on their ability: "I'm not very good at this." They blamed others for their difficulties. "It seems like you're switching on me," one student said to a research assistant. For this PG student, her struggle must be someone else's fault. Unsurprisingly, PG students demonstrated the emotional distress typical during a step-4 retreat. "My stomach hurts," one student complained; another predicted, "I'm going to hate this part" (Elliott & Dweck, 1988, p. 10).

Equally predictably, LG students maintained an even emotional keel. Instead of blaming and complaining, they concentrated on their efforts.

As we contemplate these results, we should recall that the phrases "LG students" and "PG students" describe different *behaviors*, not different *spe-

cies. In this study, Elliott and Dweck nudged students into these different categories by encouraging them to adopt different goals. Students who focus on LGs in these circumstances might well focus on PGs in others. All of us have both kinds of goals. We might habitually emphasize one kind of goal over another, but no one lives entirely in one goal world.

CLASSROOM STRATEGIES AT STEP 2

At both S3 and S2, we want our students leaning toward the right side of figure 2.1. How can we nudge them in that direction?

Our conversion toolkit includes an admirably straightforward solution. If we want our students to believe that most people struggle before they succeed, we can *tell them* that "most people struggle before they succeed." As they come to interpret setbacks as a normal part of learning, they don't fear making mistakes and respond to them with genuine determination. In brief, students who believe that school typically includes difficulties lean toward learning goals.

Catherine Good's research team explored this approach by working with middle-schoolers in Texas (Good, Aronson, & Inzlicht, 2003). For this study, seventh graders worked with college students who had been trained in different mentoring strategies. One group of mentors focused on the unique difficulties of junior high. They reminded their mentees that seventh grade includes more challenging academic work, larger classes with different teachers, and increasingly complex social networks. According to graphs that these mentors provided, seventh graders often averaged in the C range, whereas eighth graders might move into the A range. Mentors also fessed up to the difficulties that they themselves faced during this transition: difficulties that sooner or later gave way to successes.

In all these ways, one mentoring group emphasized that junior high challenges most students and that—in time—these students typically acclimate and do just fine. Thus, seventh graders learned that "many students erroneously conclude that they are not capable of high academic achievement when, in fact, the difficulties they experience are more likely due to the novelty of the situation" (Good, Aronson, & Inzlicht, 2003, p. 654).

What happened as a result of this mentoring strategy? Seventh graders in a control group averaged an 84.4 on the statewide reading test. Those who learned that struggle often precedes success averaged an 89.6. Because they knew that their struggles resembled those of other students—and even of their college mentors—they worried less about setbacks and learned to read better.

Teachers reasonably worry that by *predicting* struggle we might *cause* the very problem we're trying to prevent. We fear that all this talk of C averages and stressful peer relationships will lower grades and damage friendships. However, we should notice a key part of this strategy: the stories that Good's mentors told always concluded with success. Difficult academic work ultimately produced more learning as well as higher grades. Friendship muddles led to enduring relationships. These flights might include turbulence, but they always end with a safe landing in a better city.

Because this strategy strives to help students see struggle as normal, the technique is called *normalizing struggle*. In *Learning Begins*, we examined the working memory benefits of normalizing struggle (Watson, 2017). This technique, it seems, frees up working memory to focus on useful cognition, rather than on the internal monologue of self-doubt that can plague students. Rather than thinking, "I can't believe I just did that dumb thing; clearly I'm just not cut out for this work," our students think, "I can't believe . . . oh, wait: my teacher said that mistakes will happen, and that I'll learn from them. Maybe I just learned something?" This LG perspective reduces stress and frees up cognitive space for learning.

Of course, teachers have many opportunities to normalize struggle. Researchers have explored several of them.

Perhaps, a group of scholars reasoned, students hear too much about the effortless accomplishments of famous practitioners: the "natural talent" of Virginia Woolf or Alvin Ailey or Gabriel García Márquez (Lin-Siegler, Ahn, Chen, Fang, & Luna-Lucero, 2016). In particular, Lin-Siegler's team worried that the mini-biographies included in textbooks present famous scientists in an unhelpfully positive light. To test this hypothesis, they worked with several hundred ninth- and tenth-grade science students.

One group read traditional, success-focused histories of famous scientists. The first biography, for example, noted:

> By the time she reached college, Marie Curie was able to understand five languages: Polish, Russian, German, French, and English—all of which were the major languages that top scientists spoke at the time. Curie attended the top college in France, the Sorbonne. Not only was she the first woman to receive a degree in physics there, she was also selected for a prestigious award when she graduated.

A second biography focused on the difficulties inherent in scientific research:

> It was frustrating that many experiments ended up in failure; however, Curie would not let herself stay sad for too long. Instead, she returned to where things did not work out and tried again. Often working hour after hour and day after

day, Curie focused on solving challenging problems and learning from her mistakes. She knew that the way of progress was never easy, and later, she said, "I never yield to any difficulties."

The third biography focused not on research struggles but on scientists' personal struggles:

> Going to college was hard for Curie because at that time, people did not approve of women going to school. Thus, Curie had to study at secret classes. What's worse, when the government of Russia controlled Poland, no schools in Poland were allowed to accept any women. For this reason, Curie had to travel to another country, France, to receive education. (Lin-Siegler, Ahn, Chen, Fang, & Luna-Lucero, 2016, p. 320)

Once students understood that renowned scientists—like Curie, Faraday, and Einstein—routinely struggled, they could reasonably expect their own studies would include downs as well as ups. If Einstein didn't get it right the first time, why should they? Instead of expecting immediate perfection (PGs), they should expect slip-ups and temporary vexations before ultimate success (LGs).

Six weeks later, Lin-Siegler's team found a slight—but statistically significant—difference in these students' grades. The likeliest explanation: simply hearing that famous scientists had struggled realigned these students' goals and boosted their learning.

At least two insights help explain why the difference in grades—although measurable—was small. First, these stories produced the greatest benefit for students with relatively low grades. Those at the higher end of the grade curve didn't get as much benefit; after all, they were already doing very well. Quite possibly they were already pursuing LGs and didn't need this nudge.

Second, Lin-Siegler's strategy pursues a remarkably indirect path. Rather than teaching students more science, she instead told them different stories *about* scientists. Students who got one kind of story—but not another kind—changed their thinking about their own abilities. This readjustment in turn helped them adopt LGs and to bounce back more resiliently when they struggled. Remarkably, this causal chain produced an effect *after only six weeks*.

And it produced that effect even though the ninth and tenth graders weren't studying the work of Curie, Einstein, or Faraday. Simply knowing that famous scientists overcame real obstacles—personal and academic—helped motivate these students to learn science unrelated to that work.

MBE principle #1 tells us not simply to "do this thing" but to "think this way." Catherine Good's strategy—all those warnings, all those graphs—

might sound altogether too stern for your students or for you. Just because Good's mentors did so doesn't mean you have to.

One teacher I know contemplated Good's strategy and settled on this formula instead: "Tonight's homework will give you a chance to show me what you can do when you wrestle with complex material." This teacher didn't simply parrot a formula developed by psychologists. Instead, she found the language that worked best for her students and herself.

As we contemplate our own classrooms, both the *stories we tell* and the *tactics we embrace* make classroom challenges feel normal, even fun.

THE ART OF THE STORY

Research by Good, Lin-Siegler, and others points to a consistent conclusion: *stories matter*. When we tell students about early embarrassments that turned into triumphs, we help them rethink the very purpose of attending school. These stories fall into several categories: famous people, adults, other students, and the students' earlier selves.

Famous people have often prevailed despite discouragement and setback. Whether you talk about Thomas Edison, Toni Morrison, Alvin Ailey, Tom Brady, or Mia Hamm, you can give your students models of now-celebrated people who succeeded only after a long and difficult slog.

We can also tell more personal stories about *ourselves or our adult friends and colleagues.*

- If you failed an early calculus class before going on to major in physics, your students would benefit from your example.
- If your spouse looked up the spelling of certain words—is it "preceed" or "precede"? "proceed" or "procede"?—for years before figuring out a mnemonic, students will be happy to know they're not alone.
- If a colleague didn't get into any of his first-choice colleges and then transferred to an Ivy League school after rocking his freshman GPA, his story exemplifies academic grit.
- If you don't understand everything about a story you're teaching, you can share your puzzlement with your students.

In high school, for example, my English teacher Mr. Scott introduced our class to Flannery O'Connor's famous story "A Good Man Is Hard to Find." This curious story includes many puzzles. Why does the tone veer so strangely from comic to gothic? What does The Misfit's enigmatic final sentence mean? And—oddest of all—why on earth is there a monkey chained to a tree at Red Sammy's barbecue? Really: a monkey? It has *nothing whatsoever* to do with the story.

Mr. Scott had answers for those first two questions. And yet, he never did answer the question about the monkey. He frankly admitted he had no idea. He felt certain that it must have a greater significance. O'Connor takes too much care with her stories simply to lob in a quirky but meaningless detail. What that significance might be, however, Mr. Scott had yet to figure out. He hoped that one of us would unearth it for him.

Mr. Scott had many strengths as a teacher. His students enjoyed his classes because we wanted to know things the way Mr. Scott knew things.

At the same time, his *lack of knowledge* as much as his conspicuous knowledge helped his students love thinking about books. If someone with as much experience and wisdom as Mr. Scott *didn't know* and *wanted to know*, then we could all join in his quest to try out new interpretations. As your computer repairman would say: his confusion wasn't a bug; it was a feature.

If we take care to preserve our students' anonymity and dignity, we can also use *peers' struggles and triumphs* to reshape current students' motivation.

- "I've kept that map on the wall because it's the most beautiful student-drawn map I've ever seen. And here's a true story: at the beginning of that unit, the student who made it had the lowest score on the geography quiz in the class. You can imagine how proud he was of the progress he made. Let me tell you how he did it."
- "I had a student once break down in tears because she was so embarrassed about her French accent. She now runs a tour company in Paris—for French people."
- "It takes years to get bunting just right. We had an MVP on this team several years ago who didn't lay down a successful bunt until the second-to-last game of her senior year."

A teacher once told me a story about a sophomore—let's call her "Lupe"—whose first language was Spanish, not English. She was very quiet in class, not sure she understood what her classmates were saying, and entirely sure she couldn't contribute to the discussion. Because of her weak academic background, her analytical writing lacked many of the basics. Relying on the teacher's rewrite policy, she scraped by with precarious Cs.

Lupe might have been quiet. She might have been uncertain. But she wasn't daunted by hard work. She returned to that teacher's class as a junior and then again for two senior electives. She developed the knack of interpretation and pushed herself to try risky ones—ideas that hadn't been introduced in class and preapproved by her peers. She put in the thoughtful practice necessary to master complex sentence forms: subordinate clauses, appositives, even parallelism. She checked (and triple-checked) to ensure that she got sophisticated terminology just right. In her senior year, Lupe turned in A paper after A paper: each one a perceptive and lively read. She didn't exactly love interpreting English literature. But she worked at it and won a well-deserved reputation for insight and elegance.

As long as other students have no way of knowing Lupe's real identity, her story might well help them set their sights on long-term learning rather than short-term perfection. The more experience that you have as a teacher, the more stories like these you'll have to share with your students.

Finally, we can help students see that learning typically includes setbacks by *comparing them to themselves*.

A departmental colleague practices a kind of teacherly jujitsu in this category. Knowing that February is the cruelest month—so much Connecticut snow, so little vacation in sight—she arrives at a mid-month class with a mysterious stack of papers. With a flourish, she gives the students the very first essay they had written for her earlier in the year.

Dramatic caterwauling ensues. Her students see dreadful mistake upon dreadful mistake: sentences enfeebled by weak verbs, paragraphs disorganized by woozy topic sentences, arguments hobbled by trivial examples. They can hardly bear looking at such dreck and ask her plaintively why she has embarrassed them this way.

She smiles serenely.

"Remember," she says, "when you turned these essays in, you were quite proud of them. It was the beginning of the year, and you really wanted to impress me. This was your very best work. And now . . . *see how much progress you have made*!

"Here's the key point: we've got lots more to learn this term. But you can approach that work knowing how much you've grown already."

You can, of course, adapt this strategy to almost any class. Mathematical processes that felt daunting in the fall become automatic by December. Habits of historical analysis that once took all of a student's concentration now take place unconsciously. The picture book they labored over in the fall now feels lightheartedly easy. By holding onto work from the beginning of the year and reintroducing it to your students at just the right time, you use the example of their own obvious progress to make learning goals vivid and realistic.

You might pause right now to consider: which kind of story—better yet, which story in particular—will work best for your students, your curriculum, and you? Is there a now-famous singer who struggled at your school? Do you have a friend who, after years of indifference, morphed into a dinosaur aficionado? What topic vexed your students in November that now—in March—they have obviously mastered? How can you remind them of their progress most memorably? The time you take to consider answers—and to write them down—will make next week's teaching easier.

CULTURE OF ERROR

Stories of stumbles that turn into triumphs set a clear classroom tone. At the same time, specific teaching practices can go beyond those stories.

Doug Lemov's *Teach Like A Champion, 2.0* (2015) offers many effective teacherly strategies, including several that normalize struggle. Echoing the flowchart at the beginning of chapter 1 (figure 1.1), Lemov emphasizes that schools work best when students make mistakes and learn from them.

For that reason, he writes, we should be careful not to respond overdramatically to either event. When a student gets something wrong, we can move right away toward helping him solve the problem: "Let's try that again, Noah. What's the first thing we have to do?" (Lemov, 2015, p. 222). In this example, the teacher doesn't dwell at length on the mistake itself: "That's the same mistake you made yesterday!" Instead, this response moves immediately to discover a better approach to the question. Because mistakes are normal, we have no need to make a big deal out of them.

So, too, with correct answers. In Lemov's view, teachers don't need to ladle out compliments too zealously because getting answers right—like getting answers wrong—is all in a day's work. Simply put, "teachers [should] show their students they expect both right and wrong to happen by not making too big a deal of either" (Lemov, 2015, p. 223).

Another of Lemov's techniques accomplishes the same goal. Whenever students get an answer incorrect, we should ensure that—relatively promptly—they get the answer right. In your American history class, a discussion of the U.S. Constitution might go like this:

You: Under today's Constitution, how many terms can the president serve?

Franklin: There is no limit.

You: Ah, but an amendment created a limit. How many terms?

George: Two terms.

You: And which amendment created that limit?

Harry: The Twenty-second Amendment.

You: Correct. Franklin: which amendment created a limit of how many terms?

Franklin: The Twenty-second Amendment created a two-term limit.

You: Good.

In this exchange, Franklin got the answer wrong and then almost immediately got the answer right. Because you didn't make a big fuss about either result—both are perfectly normal—Franklin gets the clear message that learning includes mistakes.

Especially for older students, this technique might seem demeaning. Franklin got the answer right, but his answer—quite obviously—simply repeated those of George and Harry. As is so often true with Lemov's techniques, the benefit lies in the delivery. A patronizing or belittling tone, of course, will spoil the effect. Used directly and neutrally, however, it conveys a clear message: "In this classroom, our discussions quite typically include both correct and incorrect answers. We all learn from each other. That's what we do here."

Lemov frequently posts videos of teachers using his techniques. A recent example can be found here—teachlikeachampion.com/blog/masterful-no-opt-denarius-frazier-video/—and you can no doubt find many others. When you watch this technique in action, you may be surprised to see a once-mistaken student absorbing information with a hint of pleasure. He knows what he got wrong; he now knows the correct answer; he's glad to have made clear progress. In this video, this student ends up explaining his original mistake quite cogently.

Another teacher—Leah Alcala—describes a technique she calls "my favorite no" (www.teachingchannel.org/video/class-warm-up-routine). She often begins class by passing out index cards and having her eighth-grade math students solve a problem written on the board. She collects their cards, quickly sorts through them, and finds the best *incorrect* answer. She then has her students discuss that "favorite no."

Wisely, Alcala begins by having her students look for the answer's successes. Perhaps this answer multiplies by a negative number correctly. Perhaps it navigates an order-of-operations monsoon just right. Perhaps it recalls a less-than-common strategy to find the right answer. Having located its strengths, students then highlight the mistake embedded within them.

This strategy sends several beneficial messages.

- By starting most classes this way, Alcala emphasizes that mistakes happen every day. They don't surprise or upset her. Instead, the "best," "favorite" ones strike her as useful.
- Alcala dwells on a mistake's successes. The answer on an index card might be wrong, but it resulted primarily from correct—even clever—mathematical operations along the way.

- As in Lemov's technique, the student who made this mistake almost immediately learns the correct answer. Having gotten something wrong, the student quickly learns how to get it right. He gets the clear message: in school, we make progress.
- Finally, Alcala's technique separates the mistake from the person. Rather than focusing on *Martha's* mistake, the conversation centers on the mistake itself. Recalling Dweck's earlier distinction between person praise and effort praise, this technique shifts attention off the person and to the math work they're all doing.

To get the most out of this technique, you might spend some time before you use it deciding on criteria to select your "favorite mistakes." Mistakes that highlight a common misunderstanding, that occur relatively frequently, or that would be correct answers in similar circumstances all seem likely candidates to be your favorites. Your teacherly experience will guide you as you make this list.

As MBE principle #2 says, you should not simply imitate Alcala. Instead, you should translate her insight into your own idiom.

- You might conspicuously look forward to mistakes: "I hope everyone got something wrong, so we'll all have a chance to learn today."
- You might (humorously) bemoan complete success. Dweck, for example, encourages this response to error-free homework: "I apologize for wasting your time. Let's do something you can really learn from" (Dweck, 2006, p. 179).
- You might highlight your own mistakes. At a recent talk with high-school students, an Estonian student interrupted me to point out that I had misspelled "Tallinn," her country's capital. After a moment of surprised scrambling, I (thankfully) recognized the opportunity she had handed me: "If you hadn't pointed that out, I would have made that mistake over and over. Now I bet I'll always spell 'Tallinn' correctly!"

One other strategy to normalize struggle has gained currency in recent years and merits a brief discussion.

In her well-known book *Mathematical Mindsets*, Jo Boaler describes a workshop she led for math teachers. "One of the highlights of that first workshop was when Carol Dweck met with the teachers and said something that amazed them: 'Every time a student makes a mistake in math, they grow a synapse.' There was an audible gasp in the room as teachers realized the significance of this statement" (Boaler, 2016, p. 11).

The teachers might well have gasped for a different reason: *the statement is untrue*. Synapses just don't work like that. (The neurobiology of synapse formation will be described in *Learning Thrives*, the next book of this series.)

Certainly mistakes in math (and all other kinds of learning) shape chemical reactions at synapses. Teachers should know that *getting answers correct* also shapes chemical reactions at synapses. All our experiences—good, bad, and indifferent—re-sculpt neural responses to future events.

In her own book *Mindset*, Dweck describes synapse development this way: "When you learn new things, tiny connections in the brain actually multiply and get stronger. The more that you challenge your mind to learn, the more your brain cells grow" (Dweck, 2006, p. 219). This description fits the reality of synapse formation much more accurately. It can easily be adapted to help normalize struggle: "These tiny connections improve when you get something right *and* when you learn from your mistakes!"

The precise words to use will depend on your students' age and interests. Whatever phrases we use, we should—as teachers—always strive to describe brains and learning as accurately as we can. We can do better than "grow a synapse."

Figure 2.2 gathers together the solutions we've explored so far. By normalizing struggle—through the stories we tell and the errors we embrace—we encourage students to revel in the mistakes that come naturally with learning. When we do, they're less likely to run away from a challenge and much likelier to *charge!*

46   *Chapter Two*

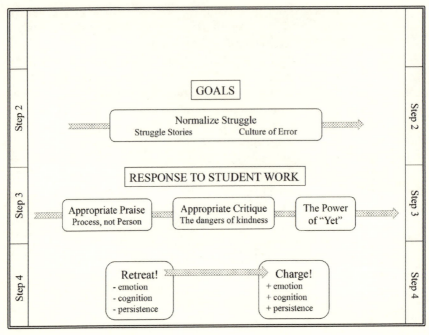

Figure 2.2.   Step 2 Solutions

Chapter Three

The First Step (at Last)

Here's our chronology so far:

1960s: psychologists found that cognitive struggle paradoxically *enhances* learning and *demotivates* many students. How can we fix this mess?

1970s: Diener and Dweck showed that students' *explanations for their struggle* matter. Students who emphasize their S3 strategic effort *charge* when facing S4 struggle. Those who concentrate on their ability, by contrast, *retreat*. This understanding leads to several concrete teaching suggestions, especially around the feedback we give our students.

1980s: Mueller and Dweck showed that students' step 2 *goals* in school matter. Those who want to perform their current knowledge typically retreat. Those who want to learn more charge. Here again, their insight offers several teaching suggestions.

In the 1990s, Dweck wanted to understand where steps 2 and 3 come from. That is, why do some students concentrate on effort, whereas others concentrate on ability? Why do some students have performance goals and others learning goals?

She wanted to find her way back to step 1.

Dweck's proposed step 1 provides a vocabulary that has shaped discussions of teaching and learning for the past decade. And, of course, it offers a host of teaching suggestions of its own.

STEP 1: THE MINDSET SOURCE

After twenty-five years of thinking and researching, Dweck arrived at the hypothesis for which she is best known. She wondered if students' *beliefs about the nature of intelligence itself* (S1) might shape both their goals in school

(S2) and their explanations for struggle (S3). Of course, if step 1 leads to steps 2 and 3, then it naturally shapes step 4: students' responses to the inevitable and beneficial difficulty of school.

Dweck reasoned this way. On the one hand, a student might believe that she has a *certain amount of intelligence and that it simply won't change*.

The belief that her intelligence is fixed (S1) might lead her to performance goals (S2). Because she can't get any smarter, after all, she naturally strives to demonstrate the intelligence she currently has.

Likewise, this S1 belief might influence a student's explanation for struggle (S3). If no amount of work can make her smarter—after all, intelligence just doesn't change—then she has no reason to focus on effort. Only ability matters.

On the other hand, a student might believe that *her level of intelligence can increase over time*.

The belief that her intelligence can grow (S1) might lead her to learning goals (S2). Because she can get smarter, she naturally sees school as the best place to strive in that direction.

Likewise, this belief might shape her explanation for struggle (S3). Given that her intelligence can change, a lack of effort and concentration can best explain her current difficulties. Ability simply doesn't present a meaningful hindrance.

Over time, Dweck named the first belief a *fixed mindset* (FM) and the second a *growth mindset* (GM) (Dweck & Sorich, 1999; Dweck, 2006; if you're interested in the history of terminology here, check out the FAQs in chapter 4).

A series of three fascinating studies (Hong, Chiu, Dweck, Lin, & Wan, 1999) provides early support for Dweck's mindset hypothesis.

Hong's First Study: S1 and S3

In their first study, Hong used a questionnaire develop by Dweck to sort undergraduates into two groups. One group, the FM students, largely agreed with statements like "You have a certain amount of intelligence and you really can't do much to change it" or "You can learn new things, but you can't really change your basic intelligence" (Hong et al., 1999, p. 590). GM students, of course, disagreed. (Those in the middle weren't included in Hong's analysis.)

Hong hypothesized that students' mindsets would influence their response to cognitive setback. To know for sure, she needed them to experience such a setback. Here's what she did.

Hong created a test that claimed to measure cognitive ability. When students got their results on that test, a "problem with the computer program" caused the printout to show both their own scores and those of another student. According to this printout—which, by the way, did not show their actual results—the student scored 64 percent. However, the "other student" whose score appeared on the page "by accident" scored 97 percent. By this method, Hong caused the students to think they had stumbled badly on a test where other students did quite well.

The research team then asked the students to explain the factors that contributed to their (relatively low) score. GM students said that their effort mattered as much as their actual conceptual ability. FM students said that their actual ability was twice as important as the effort that they put into the test. Effort just didn't matter very much for those with a fixed mindset, whereas it mattered a lot to those with a growth mindset.

In this way, Hong's first study begins to put the pieces together: *students' mindsets (S1) predict their explanations for struggle (S3).*

Hong's Second Study: S1 and S4

If Dweck is right, mindset should also predict *responses to struggle (S4)*. We would expect GM students to charge after failure, while FM students retreat.

Hong's second study tested this hypothesis by interviewing college students in Hong Kong—where English proficiency is very important in college.

Researchers told students about a remedial course in English, one that "had been shown to be effective in improving university students' English proficiency" (Hong et al., 1999, p. 593). They asked students to rate their interest level in taking such a course. They also had students fill out Dweck's mindset questionnaire.

Hong and Dweck hypothesized that GM students—especially those who struggled with English—would charge: that is, they would want to take the remedial course. On the other hand, FM students—even those who struggled with English—would retreat: that is, they would decline a course "shown to be effective" in an essential subject.

These predictions came true. For students already comfortable with English, mindset didn't really matter. Because they understood English well, they were only moderately interested in a remedial course.

For students who struggled with English, mindsets mattered a great deal. Those with a GM were quite keen to brush up their skills. However, those with a FM mostly shrugged. They were not meaningfully more interested in the class than their peers who already knew English well.

Among struggling students, a GM predicted a desire to work harder, while a FM predicted a tacit admission of defeat.

Hong's Third Study: Beyond Correlation to Causality

For her third act, Hong wanted to show that mindsets in fact *caused* the response to struggle. Her first two studies had demonstrated a correlation between the two. But perhaps the response to struggle (S4) caused the mindset (S1)—or perhaps both ways of thinking were caused by a third factor (S?).

To test a causal relationship, Hong's team developed a subtle way to influence the students' mindsets. Sixty students were asked to read and summarize a passage, ostensibly as an English comprehension measure. Half of the students read an article—designed to look like it came from *Psychology Today*—arguing that 88 percent of intelligence is genetically determined (i.e., doesn't change). To match this FM group, the other half read a GM article saying that intelligence results from the environment (i.e., does change).

All the students took a (fake) test of cognitive ability. Half of them were randomly given a satisfactory score, whereas the other half were given an unsatisfactory score: the twentieth percentile! When given a chance to take a tutorial designed to improve their scores, what did they do?

Of course, teachers think there is a desirable choice. We want all our students and *especially those at the twentieth percentile* to spend time with the tutorial. They clearly need the help!

The students who had been prompted to adopt a GM did exactly that. Seventy-three percent of them—those with the low score and even those with the higher score—signed up to do extra cognitive work. They responded to struggle by charging. That's motivation.

Students who had been prompted to adopt a FM followed a different path. Those who had the satisfactory score signed up 67 percent of the time: almost as much as those with a GM. But those who had the lower score—in other words, *those who really needed the tutorial*—signed up only 13 percent of the time.

The raw numbers here might help visualize this effect. Fifteen GM students were assigned a low score, and *eleven* of them wanted the tutorial. Fifteen FM students were assigned a low score, and *two* of them wanted the tutorial. The nine-student difference between these two groups may have a kind of poignancy because you may well be able to picture those nine students in your own class: the nine who—despite their obvious potential—simply give up when new work gets uncomfortably hard.

Because of this study design, we can in fact infer causality. By prompting a GM, Hong caused students to charge. By prompting a FM, she caused them to retreat. On figure 3.1, we can draw lots of new causal arrows.

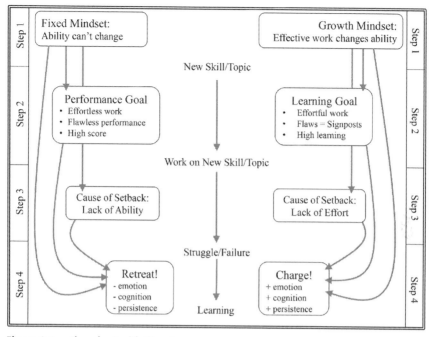

Figure 3.1. Flowchart with Step 1

This study and others like it give us many reasons to celebrate. We can now resolve the paradox first identified in the 1960s because we know where to start exploring motivation.

Rather than focus on students' cranky behavior—"Do we have to do this now?"—we recognize that S4 retreat for what it is: the *result* of several prior steps. We know to look behind that behavior for the mindsets (S1), goals (S2), and explanations for struggle (S3) that precede it.

And—more than most teachers in the country—we know that "mindsets" are but one step in this complex process. If we focus solely on that first step, as so many do, we've missed essential information. By expanding our vision to include students' goals and explanations, we can spot more clues and more opportunities to help our retreaters charge.

Grading Mindsets

To be thoroughly persuasive, Dweck's theory would benefit from two additional kinds of evidence.

First: *grades*. If GMs enhance learning and FMs undermine it, people with GMs should learn more.

To explore this prediction, we need to change our methods. Up to this point, our researchers have focused on students' cognitive and emotional behavior over the course of an hour or two. To see differences in students' *learning*, we need to track them for considerably longer periods of time.

Lisa Blackwell did just that and came up with a dramatic answer (Blackwell, Trzesniewski, & Dweck, 2007). For five years(!), Blackwell gathered data from students entering seventh grade at a public school in New York City. She and her team measured steps 1–4: the students' mindsets, their goals, their explanations for struggle, and their responses to it. And she kept track of their math grades during seventh and eighth grade.

Unlike other research projects, this one didn't try to change the students in any way. Blackwell didn't have the students read passages that encouraged them to adopt a GM. She didn't have them think they had failed at a logic puzzle. She simply measured what they already believed and then connected those measurements to their academic development.

The FM students made no progress in math. Halfway through seventh grade, they averaged just over a 71; at the end of eighth grade, just under a 71. Their grades barely budged—and to the degree that they did, they budged down.

On the other hand, the average grade for the GM students rose gradually and steadily. Halfway through seventh grade they averaged a 73. When they finished eighth grade, that number had risen to just under 76. As seen in figure 3.2, a two-point gap in seventh grade turned into a five-point gap at the end of eighth.

(In this graph, Blackwell uses the label "Incremental" for students with a growth mindset and "Entity" for those with a fixed mindset. This odd nomenclature, quite common in early research, is explained in chapter 4's FAQs.)

Note that both the FM and GM students lived in the same community, attended the same school, ate the same food, used the same textbooks, and—presumably—liked the same music (that their parents and teachers thought was dreadful). In fact, they all had the same math teacher. The most plausible explanation for the grade divergence is not external circumstances but internal motivation. Students who believed they could change their intelligence at S1 pursued learning goals at S2, explained their struggles by looking inward at S3, and worked harder when the math proved a challenge at S4. In this way, their GM motivated them to learn more.

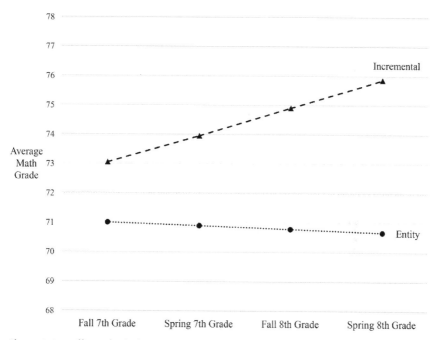

Figure 3.2. Effect of Mindset on Middle School Math Grades. *Adapted from "Implicit Theories of Intelligence Predict Achievement Across an Adolescent Transition: A Longitudinal Study and an Intervention," by L. S. Blackwell, K. H. Trzesniewski, & C. S. Dweck, 2007, Child Development, 78(1), p. 251. Copyright 2007 by John Wiley & Sons, Inc. Reprinted with permission.*

In other words: mindset theory isn't some cute academic trick that produces results in psychology labs. Mindsets shape students' motivation and thereby shape their learning.

Research at all grade levels—not just seventh—finds that a GM boosts learning. Valanne Henderson reached that conclusion when she studied the transition to middle school (Henderson & Dweck, 1990). So did Deborah Stipek when she studied third through sixth graders (Stipek & Gralinski, 1996). So did Daeun Park, working with students as young as fifth and second grade (Park, Gunderson, Tsukayama, Levine, & Beilock, 2016).

Research with college students tells the same story in a different language. Imagine two groups of students: group A has higher SAT scores than group B. History tells us that group A ought to have a higher college GPA as well. (That's why colleges care about SAT scores; they predict GPA.)

If, instead, both groups had the same GPA, you would wonder: what's wrong with group A? Why isn't their SAT advantage turning into a GPA advantage? They seem to be paying some mysterious cognitive tax.

Richard Robins and Jennifer Pals identified this tax when they tracked more than five hundred college students at the University of California, Berkeley (2002). In their research, FM students had higher average SAT scores than GM students but the same average GPA. For these FM students, a high SAT did not yield a high GPA. Their FM taxed their accomplishment.

This conclusion applies not only to different ages but also to different groups of learners. In a study done for the Brookings Institution, Susana Claro and Susanna Loeb (2017) looked at data covering 125,000 third-through eighth-grade students in California schools. Yes: *one hundred and twenty-five thousand.*

Like other scholars, they found that GMs help students learn. They also found that GMs help boys *and* girls learn. They help students who speak English as a native language *and* those who learn it in school. They help students from all income brackets. They help students in special education classes. Given the extraordinary number of students included in their analysis, we've got good reason to be confident in their findings.

∼

In brief: mindsets don't simply influence students' choices when it comes to signing up for hypothetical college courses. They shape student learning.

∼

The Neuroscience of Mindset

All these studies into mindsets' effects on grades give us strong reasons to believe Dweck's hypothesis. Another kind of evidence would persuade us still further.

Teachers can, all too easily, conflate psychology and neuroscience. Both disciplines study the brain, it seems, so we can think of them as basically the same thing.

This common misconception, however, overlooks crucial differences. Neuroscience studies *brains*; that is, it studies *physical objects*. Neuroscientists look at cells—their development, the electrical and chemical connections among them, the blood that flows around them.

Psychology studies *minds*; that is, the *behavior of that physical object*. How do people learn? When do we pay attention? What motivates us?

For example: when neuroscientists want to study the effects of stress on learning, they stress out a mouse and then look at changes to cells in its hippocampus. When psychologists want to study the effects of stress on learning, they stress out a mouse and then measure its ability to learn a new maze. One group studies things; the other studies the *behavior* of things.

These fields complement each other, but they offer meaningfully different ways of thinking about teaching and learning.

Dweck's work rests squarely in psychology. She and her colleagues are not looking at cell behavior in people's brains but at mental actions in people's minds. Their work would be all the more convincing if we could find support in neuroscience as well. Does a FM produce one set of neural patterns, whereas a GM produces a distinct set?

Right away, we must be very careful about asking this question. We don't want to say there is a "mindset part of the brain." That kind of thinking is both common and overly simplistic. We also don't want to suggest that observed brain differences somehow suggest some people are "hardwired" to be FM whereas others are "hardwired" to be GM. As we've already seen, Hong prompted people to adopt a FM or a GM simply by reading a fake psychology article. (And the belief that people are "hardwired" is itself a kind of FM.)

Instead, neuroscientists can make some informed predictions. If mindset theory is true, we can anticipate how brains ought to react when they are in GM mode and how they would instead react in FM mode. If those predictions come true, then we can have even greater confidence in Dweck's theory. Using strikingly different methodologies, two distinct fields of brain science would have found corroborating evidence.

Dweck worked with Columbia University neuroscientist Jennifer Mangels to undertake such an investigation (Mangels, Butterfield, Lamb, Good, & Dweck, 2006). Using Dweck's mindset questionnaires, Mangels identified FM and GM thinkers among a group of Columbia undergraduates. These students then sat at a computer to answer challenging factual questions: for example, "What is the capital of Oman?" If they got the answer wrong—in this case, if they typed in anything other than "Muscat"—they were given the correct answer.

While doing all this work at the computer, these students wore a gizmo ("electroencephalogram array") that measured electrical activity on the outermost layer of the brain. In this way, Mangels and Dweck could see areas of heightened neural activity at different points in the task. In particular, they wanted to know how brains reacted (a) when they saw that they had gotten the answer wrong and (b) when they heard the correct answer to the question.

Mangles and Dweck predicted that FM students would get hung up on the fact that they didn't know the capital of Oman. Internally, these students would be saying to themselves, "I got it wrong! I got it wrong!" over and over. On the other hand, they predicted that GM students would work on processing the correct answer. For them, getting things wrong isn't such a tragedy, and so instead they would repeat to themselves, "Muscat! Muscat! Muscat!"

To test this hypothesis, the researchers looked at a region of the brain that typically reacts when it detects errors. (If brain geography is interesting to you, it's called the "anterior cingulate cortex": the ACC.) Sure enough, at the moment FM thinkers saw they had gotten it wrong, they produced considerably higher activity levels in the ACC than the GM thinkers. Alarm bells were going off at the brain's midline.

Mangels and Dweck also looked at a region of the brain that processes linguistic information. (It's just under your left temple, in the "left temporal lobe.") Here again, results confirmed the researchers' predictions. GM thinkers activated left temporal lobe networks considerably more than FM thinkers did because they were processing correct answers.

As a final piece of evidence, students were—surprise!—retested on all the questions they had gotten wrong the first time. Sure enough, the amount of left-temporal-lobe processing predicted the likelihood that the students learned the new information.

GM students didn't get hung up on making mistakes, so their ACC remained relatively quiet. Instead, they focused on processing new information, so they engaged left-temporal-lobe networks. And that increased information processing led to greater learning.

Today, many Columbia graduates know the capital of Oman because they went into this study with a GM.

CLASSROOM STRATEGIES AT STEP 1

In previous chapters, we looked at S3 strategies to highlight effort and S2 strategies to convert performance goals into learning goals. What S1 strategies might translate a fixed mindset into a growth mindset?

As psychologists have explored this question, their answers have focused on the *explicit* language we use to describe intelligence and on the *implicit* messages that our classroom practices convey.

Explicit Messages

We've seen before that straightforward messages work. When we tell students that learning often requires mental struggle, they believe us. When they perceive struggle as normal, they adopt learning goals.

We might reasonably believe this approach will help directly with mindsets. If we want students to believe that the right kind of cognitive work changes intelligence, we can just tell them. If they believe us, they might learn more. Lisa Blackwell has tried just this approach.

As we've seen, Blackwell tracked five years of seventh graders to determine if mindsets influence learning. (They do.) She continued her exploration to see if *changing* a student's mindset might *improve her learning* (Blackwell et al., 2007).

Working with seventh graders who initially believed that intelligence doesn't change—that is, students with a FM—she put together an eight-week program showing that learning rewires brains. Blackwell reasoned that, as students learn how brains change, they might reasonably infer that intelligence can change. That is, they can become GM students.

At the end of the school year, she then remeasured their mindsets. She also compared their grades to a control group.

Sure enough, when these seventh graders filled out the mindset questionnaires at the end of the school year, they moved from the FM to the GM camp. Telling students that brains change and *how* brains change helped them think that intelligence can change. A curriculum that included some basic psychology and some basic neuroscience helped convert mindsets.

Equally important, the students who learned about malleable brains also *learned more math*. As we see in figure 3.3, their once-declining math grades

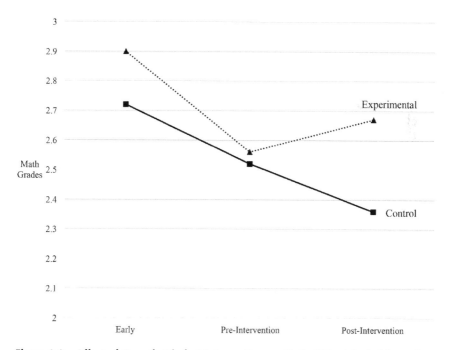

Figure 3.3. Effect of Growth Mindset Intervention on Math GPA. *Adapted from "Implicit Theories of Intelligence Predict Achievement Across an Adolescent Transition: A Longitudinal Study and an Intervention," by L. S. Blackwell, K. H. Trzesniewski, & C. S. Dweck, 2007, Child Development, 78(1), p. 257. Copyright 2007 by John Wiley & Sons, Inc. Reprinted with permission.*

started to climb. They started on a new cognitive trajectory—one that promised a more hopeful academic future.

(In this graph, the "Experimental" line shows results for students who heard that brains change, and "Control" shows the students who didn't.)

Blackwell quotes a teacher describing one student who went through this 8-week program: "M. was [performing] far below grade level. During the past several weeks, she has voluntarily asked for extra help from me during her lunch period in order to improve her test-taking performance. Her grades drastically improved from failing to an 84 [on] her recent exam" (Blackwell et al., 2007, p. 256).

In our language, when her mindset changed from fixed to growth, her S4 behavior changed from *retreat!* to *charge!*

Because we have read about so many studies by this point, we might have become blasé about this success story. However, it's worthwhile to pause and consider Blackwell's almost shocking result. This group of students learned more math, even though Blackwell *didn't teach them any math*. She didn't teach them any study strategies. She didn't give their teachers new information about cognitive processes, like working memory or attention. Blackwell's intervention was almost entirely unrelated to math or even to school. And yet, these students learned more.

A recent meta-analysis bears out Blackwell's strategy. Especially with at-risk students and especially in math, "inducing a growth mindset by teaching neuroplasticity has an overall positive effect on motivation, achievement, and brain activity" (Sarrasin, Nenciovici, Foisy, Allaire-Duquette, Riopel, & Masson, 2018, p. 22).

When students (S1) believe that intelligence can change, they (S2) reject performance goals for learning goals, (S3) focus on their own strategic efforts, and (S4) remain resilient. A change in mindset changes motivation.

Explicit (but Indirect) Messages

Another research team tried a related approach, although theirs included a sneaky twist at the end (Aronson et al., 2002).

Joshua Aronson's team gathered college students together and asked each one to write a pen-pal letter to a struggling middle schooler. Aronson's team gave specific instructions to the college students, telling them to encourage the middle schoolers to "work hard in spite of their difficulties" because "the brain is like a muscle": it grows when you exercise it (Aronson et al., 2002, pp. 117–18; for more information on this common analogy, see the FAQs).

They encouraged the college students to use their own experiences as examples of this message. In this way, Aronson ensured that the college students contemplated this GM message not only in an abstract way but with specific connections to their own lives.

After college students wrote letters to the middle schoolers, *voila!*: their own mindsets began to change. They ended that school year with considerably higher GMs than their control-group peers. Having told someone else that intelligence can grow, they believed that message even more themselves. And, impressively, their own grades went up. Students who wrote GM letters to middle-schoolers averaged a B+. Those in the control group averaged closer to a B.

From one perspective, this difference might not seem like much. Moving from a B to a B+ doesn't dramatically alter a student's life. From another perspective, that change seems extraordinary. These students wrote *one* letter to a stranger. When they encouraged a GM-approach to learning, they increased their own GM. And that simple step boosted their own learning.

We might be curious to hear about the effect these amazing GM letters had on the middle schoolers who received them. That's the sneaky twist: no students in fact got these letters. The researchers wanted to know if simply *writing* these letters would have an effect, so that's where they focused their research energy.

To be clear: Aronson's study does not imply that we ought to lie to our students and have them write letters to nonexistent pen pals. His methodology is a research strategy, not a teaching strategy. We should not imitate but *translate*.

As teachers, we can coach our students to *coach each other* in GM ways.

- Does your school have peer tutors?
- Do you have reading buddies in your classroom?
- Do you post guidelines for group work?
- Do you talk with older siblings about the best ways to mentor younger siblings?

In each of these cases and many others, the GM instructions that you give will benefit both the students being coached and the student coaches themselves. The more that they embrace a GM perspective when working with one another, the more they will understand and embrace the idea themselves.

Explicit Messages: Reveal the Secret?

The most straightforward mindset strategy goes like this: we could let our students in on the lingo. We could tell them about FMs and GMs: the perils of the first and the benefits of the second.

Many teachers use this very approach. At the beginning of a school year, social media sites host videos of adorable first graders singing growth mindset songs. At conferences, teachers swap endearing stories about students encouraging one another to adopt a GM approach. If you want to try this out for yourself, you can find plenty of guidance to help you along.

At the same time, we have reasons to hesitate.

First, we don't have any research that looks at this question directly. Ideally, a researcher would create two classroom environments. In a control group, teachers would use GM strategies *without* explicitly teaching students about mindsets. In the experimental group, teachers would *both* use the strategies *and* teach some Dweck. The hypothesis would be that combining strategies with mindset language would boost learning.

Such a study would let us know if using GM language produces any benefit beyond using GM teaching strategies. Alas, as of right now no one has done that study.

Second, this strategy creates potential perils of its own.

After all, mindset language itself is rather abstract. A teacher might say to a struggling student, "Remember how important it is to have a growth mindset!" The student might nod eagerly and perhaps hum a few bars of the mindset song.

And yet, that reminder might not turn into specific mindset behavior. After all, *adults* often struggle to apply mindset strategies in specific classroom circumstances. We might well doubt that our students know what to do with our general advice.

In other words: I might feel good that I'm doing something, but that something might not actually help students learn.

Instead, I might say, "You remember that Curie really struggled to get her experiments under way. Maybe we need a new approach. Try again, and this time you can partner with Irene." This more specific advice—normalizing struggle, offering a new avenue to solve the problem—might be likelier to create a GM and lead to more learning.

In the absence of research, we simply don't know which strategy helps more. Teachers who adopt explicit mindset language might take care to observe their students' subsequent actions. If student behavior changes, then the technique is helping. If it doesn't, it might be time to reconsider. As the classroom teacher, you get to make the ultimate decision.

Implicit Invitations

As we hone our explicit GM messages, we also know that teaching practices can implicitly promote mindsets—either fixed or growth. A true story from my graduate school days highlights this point.

On the first day of classes, I attended back-to-back lectures. In the first, a graduate student explained the course's grading philosophy: to prevent grade inflation, the average grade in the course had been fixed at a B+. Given that this was a well-known graduate school, we should all be quite proud of a B+. That grade, he assured us, indicated a very solid understanding of the material.

In this class, clearly, grades sorted the "best" students from the "solid" students and from the "less-than-solid" students. No matter how much work we did, no matter how much we actually *learned*, we would ultimately hit a predetermined ceiling. This grading policy, designed to enforce a bell curve, meant that one student's smartness required another's ignorance. My classmates' accomplishments automatically diminished my own.

In the very next lecture I attended, the professor delivered a heartfelt speech that went something like this:

> One of my great teaching regrets is that I've never successfully helped *all* my students understand the material completely. I hope that this is the year I'll succeed. I need your help in accomplishing that goal.
>
> If you understand all the material, that's wonderful! But if you're confused or struggling, *please* help me. Please bring questions to your TAs or come to my office hours or e-mail me questions after class. If you do, then everyone in the class will learn all the material, and I will finally have accomplished my goal. I'll be so pleased if everyone gets an A on the final exam! I've got a really good feeling about this year.

In this course, unlike the first, grades didn't force students into arbitrary categories. Instead, they measured how well students had learned. The professor wanted everyone to learn everything. In fact, he conspicuously believed that everyone could.

These two grading systems enact different mindsets. The first policy insists that some people are always smarter than others. Even if we all turned in equally good (or equally bad) work, our TAs would find some way to enforce distinctions among us. The second policy insists that everyone can learn everything in the course. If all students master the content (or fail to learn any of it), they'll all get the same grade.

Of course, many policies about grades, deadlines, and revisions imply mindset messages.

For example, if a teacher allows his students to revise an essay, his policy sends a clear message: "There is no such thing as *good writing*. There is only *good rewriting*." Good writers aren't born; they're made.

You can send implicit mindset messages in whichever way best fits your circumstances.

- Perhaps your students can set their own deadlines.
- You might allow them to revise work for credit.
- You might highlight your comments and downplay the grades.
- To reward learning more than speed, you might weigh later assignments more than early ones. (This strategy also ensures that we reward students who learn things, not only those who already knew them.)
- Your rubric might credit both the process students used as well as the final product.

For example, Eleanor O'Rourke devised a computer game to help students learn fractions (O'Rourke, Haimovitz, Ballweber, Dweck, & Popović, 2014). One version rewarded correct answers. The other gave additional points for useful learning behaviors: persistence, trying varied strategies, and so forth. In their study, O'Rourke found that students stayed with this second version considerably longer. That is: it was more motivating.

Lisa Blackwell's work with seventh graders shows such implicit policies in action. One of Blackwell's teachers described a student this way: "L., who never puts in any extra effort and doesn't turn in homework on time, actually stayed up late working for hours to finish an assignment early so I could review it and give him a chance to revise it. He earned a B+ on the assignment (he had been getting C's and lower)" (Blackwell et al., 2007, p. 256).

In this brief example, a combination of mindset efforts yielded impressive results. First, Blackwell's explicit GM message—"brains change when students learn"—enhanced this student's motivation. Then, the teacher's implicitly GM grading policy—a willingness to look at early drafts and allow revisions—channeled that motivation to highly effective work. Once upon a time, L had retreated: he "never put in any extra effort." With his evolving mindset and his teacher's flexibility, he started to charge.

Other researchers have found similar results.

Daeun Park's research team reviewed data from a yearlong study of first and second graders. They found that when teachers rewarded high grades and scores ("I give special privileges to students who do the best work"), their students increasingly adopted a FM. Unsurprisingly, their students learned less math over the course of the year (Park et al., 2016, pp. 304–5).

On the flip side, when Carole Ames and Jennifer Archer studied high-school classrooms, they found a beneficial correlation between teachers' grading policies and their students' mindset pathways (1988). When teachers allowed corrections and revisions, their students talked more about learning and less about test scores. They chose challenging projects over easy ones. They simply enjoyed class more.

Translating Grading Theory into Classroom Practice

Classroom teachers have strong opinions about our grading systems. Advice about grade policies and procedures can feel like a deep criticism of our work.

Objections to *revision* policies typically fall into two camps. First, practically speaking, such a policy might create an impossible work overload. Regrading updated versions of assignments would add to an already stressful burden.

Only you know your teaching life well enough to weigh this concern justly. Teachers frequently discover that, to their surprise, this practice *reorganizes* workload without increasing it. For example, if a student can rewrite an assignment often enough to fix all the run-on sentences, then she's less likely to make that mistake in the next assignment. In this example, the teacher's extra work on the first essay might reduce his work later on.

Other teachers reason that if their extra work helps students discover intrinsic motivation, then it is time well spent. Yes, it takes time to create alternate versions of tests, but you might be happy you did when your students work harder to grapple with the concept being tested.

A second objection argues that life includes deadlines and students need practice meeting them. If they learn in school that "you can always redo everything," when will they learn how to get anything done? This objection often ends this way: "There are times in life you just can't get an extension. You have to pay your taxes!"

Because this objection focuses on the philosophical more than the practical, psychology research can't address it directly. Your foundational beliefs on questions like these will shape your teaching practice. At the same time, if you're determined to promote intrinsic motivation, you might reexamine this perspective.

A GM revision policy doesn't require that students "can always redo everything." At some point, most school systems do require a final grade. Instead, such a policy would start with at least a few more opportunities for revision and at least a little more credit for improvement. For example, you might allow your students to:

- revise no more than two papers a term,
- retake quizzes but not tests, and
- revise only after they have met with a peer tutor.

Each of us can design a rewrite policy that best fits us. If we approach a revision policy not as an all-or-nothing proposition but as an adaptable set of possibilities, then it allows students to develop a GM and a sense of responsibility.

(By the way, although you do have to pay your taxes, in the United States, you can get an automatic six-month extension. If you realize you've made a mistake, you can refile updated returns years later. The standard remains the same—you do have to pay your taxes—but the actual tax deadline has lots of flexibility.)

Champions of a bell curve, like my first grad school professor, also offer both practical and philosophical arguments.

Practically speaking, a bell curve often matches classroom reality. Students start with different levels of experience and bring different levels of interest. For that reason, it's not surprising that a few earn As, a few earn Ds, and most end up in the C–B range. Given this common experience, we might struggle to imagine that all our students will learn enough to get an A. (As the optimistic professor acknowledged, he had never in his career achieved his all-A goal.)

Philosophically speaking, the idea that everyone might get an A might sound frankly unnerving. It simply abandons the standards that we have been maintaining during our careers.

GM advocates acknowledge both objections. At the same time, counseled by Dweck, they make room for an alternative perspective.

As a teacher, I'm responsible for helping my students master a particular curriculum. If, in fact, they all master it, then they should all get the highest grade. They accomplished the goal we set for them.

In reality, that's unlikely. But it is possible. And that result is much likelier if the grading policies we set encourage a GM. If—because we teach well and foster GMs—all our students *do* learn all the material, then a high class average doesn't expose low standards. Instead, it emphasizes our remarkable accomplishment.

Dweck's research rarely forbids one approach or requires another. Instead, it suggests that we rethink our options with fresh eyes.

When we take a grading path that suggests ability can change over time, we start a mental process that ultimately boosts motivation. Even if we can't always take that path, doing so occasionally will help our students learn more than doing so infrequently—or never.

Because grades have traditionally had such an important place in school, we can think of them as strategies throughout our model. At step 1, grading policies communicate implicit mindset messages. At step 2, revision policies and low-stakes assessments normalize struggle and foster a culture of error. At step 3, they give us the chance to praise and criticize appropriately. As you'll see at the end of the chapter, figure 3.4 includes grades at all three steps.

Expanding "Disciplinary" Mindsets

One final implicit GM strategy offers teachers a cornucopia of tempting possibilities. This strategy draws on Jo Boaler's contention that teachers should help math students think differently about her discipline. In this paragraph, she contrasts fixed mindset thinking and a "mathematical mindset":

> When students see math as a series of short questions, they cannot see the role for their own inner growth and learning. They think that math is a fixed set of methods that either they get or they don't. [However, when] students see math as a broad landscape of unexplored puzzles in which they can wander around, asking questions and thinking about relationships, they understand that their role is thinking, sense making, and growing. When students see mathematics as a set of ideas and relationships and their role as one of thinking about the ideas, and making sense of them, they have a mathematical mindset. (Boaler, 2016, p. 34)

Initially, this proposal sounds appealing. No doubt we want students to perceive math not as an established set of facts and procedures but as a field to explore and expand with their efforts. Relatively quickly, however, we can spot the gap in Boaler's paragraph. To highlight it, let's repeat her definition—with two words changed:

> When students see *history* as a series of short questions, they cannot see the role for their own inner growth and learning. They think that *history* is a fixed set of methods that either they get or they don't. However, when students see *history* as a broad landscape of unexplored puzzles in which they can wander around, asking questions and thinking about relationships, they understand that their role is thinking, sense making, and growing. When students see *history* as a set of ideas and relationships and their role as one of thinking about the ideas, and making sense of them, they have a *historical* mindset.

Most history teachers fervently pursue this goal. We want our students to perceive history not as an established set of facts and procedures but as a field to explore and expand with their efforts. No doubt science teachers, music teachers, and theology teachers feel the same way. Almost all teachers want students to see our fields as welcome to fresh exploration.

In other words, there is nothing especially mathematical about "mathematical mindsets." Boaler's term doesn't need revision because it's wrong but because she hasn't made her claim bold enough. We can understand her idea as a powerful expansion of Dweck's fundamental argument.

Dweck's definition focuses on a student's perception of *her own ability*. With a FM, she believes her ability can't change. With a GM, she believes it can. Boaler—quite wonderfully—suggests a new kind of mindset: one focusing not on *malleability of self* but on *malleability of academic discipline*.

Students who have what we might call a "fixed disciplinary mindset" believe that a field—math, Spanish, lacrosse, sculpture, chemistry—won't change. Everything to know about these things is already known. School exists simply as a place to dispense and absorb extant knowledge.

On the other hand, students with a "growth disciplinary mindset" believe that these fields can indeed change. In fact, they believe that their efforts might change them.

A recent conversation reminded me of this Boaler-inspired idea. I ate lunch with an eighth grader who had an eighth grader's devotion to all things outer space. He offered an impassioned description of string theory but concluded on a down note:

Robert (soberly): Of course, we can't prove any of this yet.

Me (a bit disappointed): Oh. What would we need to prove it?

Robert (blandly): We need to invent a new kind of math.

With his "growth disciplinary mindset," Robert saw inventing a new kind of math as an utterly plausible solution. In the same way he can learn the kinds of math that do exist (fractions, geometry, linear algebra), he can also create kinds of math that don't yet exist. Given (S1) his "growth disciplinary mindset," it seems likely he will (S2) approach math classes with learning goals rather than performance goals and (S3) focus on the work he puts in more than simply the math ability he has. As a result, he will (S4) charge when faced with a challenge. Result: a more intrinsically motivated student.

This suggestion invites teachers to a complex balancing act. To promote a growth disciplinary mindset (GDM), we might well encourage our students to create new things within our discipline. History teachers might have students create web pages exploring overlooked historical figures. Dance teachers might ask students to choreograph new dance steps—perhaps ones inspired by another class. A field hockey coach might invite the captains to map out a new play.

These hypotheticals, however, call for a clear-minded balance; we shouldn't assign them precisely because we need the results to be awesome.

The web pages on historical figures might very well miss both important facts and the historical context that gives them meaning. A dance inspired by a phonics lesson might look like a mess. The new field-hockey play might lead to an own-side goal.

Instead, we should create such assignments to help students re-envision our disciplines as ever-expanding fields. History and dance and field hockey aren't complete enterprises. We're adding to them every day. Scientists haven't yet unified the fields, but someday they will. We haven't yet invented the math that will prove (or disprove) string theory, but someday we will. We want our students to have growth mindsets not only about themselves but about the very fields they are studying.

To be clear: unlike other strategies discussed in this book, this suggestion doesn't have direct research support behind it. At the same time, its alignment with mindset theory overall makes it too intriguing not to include here.

DANIEL RETURNS

What does all this mindset theory have to do with my student Daniel?

As you remember from chapter 1, Daniel scored a 44 percent on the proficiency test, and I needed to motivate him to earn a 75 percent. This task struck me as all but impossible because—after all—experience taught me that some students just don't learn grammar. They're good kids, but they don't have grammar brains. Daniel and I both faced impossible tasks.

As we eyeballed those tasks, we were both lucky that I had started studying Dweck the summer before I met him. Almost immediately, I recognized Daniel's greatest handicap: when it came to grammar, his teacher had The Most Fixed Mindset Possible. Every time I told myself that "some students just don't have grammar brains," I was reinforcing to myself the fixedness of my students' intelligence.

I have subsequently recognized a specific FM habit in myself. Aneeta Rattan's work shows that FM teachers often make firm decisions about their students' abilities after just one test (Rattan et al., 2012). In this case, I had concluded that Daniel could never learn grammar *before I had even met him*.

Of course, Daniel could have been sick the day he took the proficiency test. Perhaps he'd had a fight with his parents or a significant other or his best friend. Perhaps his team had lost a big game the day before. Perhaps his sophomore English teacher didn't prepare him well for the test, or perhaps they just didn't get along. And yet, even though any one of these explanations was entirely plausible, I had skipped right over them all and immediately concluded that Daniel was unteachable.

Although my thought process at the time was wrongheaded, I do want to give my old self his due. In truth, my experience had shown me—at times quite vividly—that some students really struggle with grammar. Despite my best teaching efforts, a handful of my students just never made much progress.

And so, I faced a puzzle. Dweck's research told me to adopt a GM. Years of hard-won teaching experience taught me to have a FM about grammar. What was I to do?

Finally, following the adage, I decided to "fake it until I could make it." That is, I would pretend I believed all that mindset stuff, though, in my heart of grammarly hearts, I just didn't. I reasoned that, if Dweck were wrong and mindset didn't make any difference, the worst outcome would be that Daniel wouldn't learn any more grammar. But I already thought he wasn't going to learn, so that worst-case scenario wasn't all that bad. For me and for Daniel, Dweck's theory was an all-upside investment.

And so, I committed to using mindset strategies. I would compliment Daniel's work ("Good job that you fixed these first three gerund exercises."), not Daniel himself ("You've got the makings of a grammar genius!"). I would not be tempted by kindness to imply grammar knowledge lay outside his reach ("Grammar is really difficult for some students. Don't worry—I know all about your soccer prowess."). I would adopt GM grading policies and practices (over the year, Daniel revised *lots* of assignments).

More specifically, I committed myself to a reasonable goal. Of course, Daniel could not jump from a 44 percent to a 75 percent in one year. He barely knew any grammar to start with, so how could he make that much progress? Instead, I determined to help him get halfway there: a 60 percent felt like a reasonable GM goal. If he learned that much as a junior, he would go into his senior year confident he could learn even more.

I tell this story to offer reassurance. Sometimes a mindset discussion can be tinged with blame: "Any teacher who clings to a FM, who doesn't immediately adopt a GM, clearly isn't keeping up with all the latest research," such discussions imply. "Stop asking questions and get on board."

I myself am all in favor of asking questions about mindset research—both because we should *always* question research and because my own grammar experience raised plausible questions. This book won't blame you if you want to think over this research, to doubt its findings, to test it thoroughly and skeptically before you accept its conclusions.

By the way: what happened with Daniel?

He scored a 44 percent at the end of sophomore year. My secret goal was that he score a 60 percent at the end of his junior year. Instead, he scored a 76 percent.

The First Step (at Last)

Before I ever met Daniel, I had concluded he'd never pass the test. Eight Dweck-filled months later, he passed it with a point to spare.

I sometimes hesitate to tell this story because it might sound like I'm boasting. "See what a good teacher I am," you might hear me say.

My message, in fact, is something else entirely. I knew nothing more about grammar or grammar teaching Daniel's year than the year before. The only difference was that I knew more about fostering intrinsic motivation. I didn't need to *motivate* Daniel. I needed to redirect him away from a demotivating path. Once on that new path, he found his own way to grammar.

To be clear: *Daniel* did the extra homework. Daniel retook the quizzes. Daniel met with me for extra help and worked with a peer tutor. He did the work and he did the learning. I and my fixed mindset mostly got out of the way. Daniel's cheerful and determined efforts—abetted by Dweckified teaching—resulted in grammar mastery.

Figure 3.4 summarizes the strategies that helped Daniel make his way there.

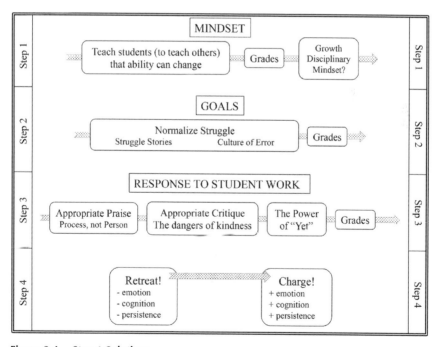

Figure 3.4. Step 1 Solutions

Chapter Four

The Mindset Controversy and FAQs

Or perhaps everything you've read so far is wrong.

Any theory as well-known as Dweck's will stir up some controversy along the way. Certainly mindset theory has faced skepticism, even criticism. During the past few years, while the field of psychology has been rocked by the "replication crisis," mindset critics have raised important concerns and objections (Camerer et al., 2018). Psychologist Nick Soderstrom even mused on Twitter about his concern that "mindset is becoming the new learning styles" (NickSoderstrom, 2018).

(Although many teachers continue to believe in learning styles theories, they have been thoroughly debunked by psychologists [Pashler, McDaniel, Rohrer, & Bjork, 2008; Willingham, 2009]. To call mindset "the new learning styles" is to dismiss it as a stubborn fad that doesn't hold up to scientific scrutiny.)

Soderstrom isn't saying that mindset theory must be rejected. He does wonder, however, if teachers should reexamine our less-than-critical embrace of the theory.

Mindset criticism falls into two camps.

INDIVIDUALS IN SOCIAL SYSTEMS

The first camp argues that the theory distracts us from bigger problems. In an article written for *Salon* magazine, Alfie Kohn worries that mindset shifts the blame away from the adults and onto the children. As he puts it, some "educators would rather convince students they need to adopt a more positive attitude than address the quality of the curriculum (what the students are being taught) or the pedagogy (how they're being taught)" (Kohn, 2015).

More broadly, in Kohn's view, mindset theory distracts us from unjust social systems by focusing on individual behavior within them:

> The message of [the American] tradition has always been to adjust yourself to conditions as you find them because those conditions are immutable; all you can do is to decide on the spirit in which to approach them. Ironically, the more we occupy ourselves with getting kids to attribute outcomes to their own effort, the more we communicate that the conditions they face are, well, fixed. (Kohn, 2015)

Although Kohn acknowledges Dweck's careful research, he decries both the way that cultural critics use her theory and her failure to rebut them. (He also doesn't much like praise: either person praise or process praise.)

If Kohn is right, we should stop distracting ourselves with mindset theory and focus instead on the curriculum, the pedagogy, and American social structure. If Kohn is right, mindset theory isn't so much wrong as irrelevant.

And yet Kohn's argument proposes a false dichotomy. We can, of course, *both* reconsider curriculum and pedagogy *and* use psychology research to foster intrinsic motivation. We can contemplate Kohn's analysis of American society and at the same time decide how best to use Dweck's insights. One choice does not preclude the other.

Kohn dismisses Dweck with a clever paradox: by promoting a growth mindset—students should "attribute outcomes to their own effort"—we imply that the social conditions they face are fixed. And yet, people who learn the value of determined, decisive action—students who "attribute outcomes to their own effort"—can in fact alter the unjust systems within which they live. History gives us many such examples, including several within the American tradition.

Part II of this book shows how an extension of mindset theory might help upend some of the social structures that Kohn criticizes.

Of course, Kohn's broader social analysis lies outside the scope of this book. You might agree or disagree with his cultural critique quite passionately. You might not spend much time worrying about such questions. Whatever the case, mindset theory doesn't necessarily conform to or support a particular social vision. We can use it to further the good work we want our students to do in life and in school.

Speaking of school—before teachers can set about changing the systems we work in, we have to function within them. You, like Kohn, might want to revolutionize your school's curriculum. You might want to promote a wholly different model of effective teaching. But, for today, you've got to motivate your students to explore the current curriculum with the current teaching methods. A clear-headed understanding of mindset can help you do just that.

This book strives not to change complex social systems, although—no doubt—many need changing. Instead, it strives to help individual teachers do our best work in the schools we currently have. If you start your students down a growth mindset path on step 1, they're likelier to take better steps 2, 3, and 4. The result will be greater intrinsic motivation, even within an imperfect curriculum, an imperfect school, an imperfect society. Our students might ultimately develop the motivation to improve all three.

THE "REPLICATION CRISIS"

The second camp of those who critique mindset theory, unlike Kohn's, focus on its scientific validity. In this second view, the theory isn't merely irrelevant but *wrong*. If you ask the questions Dweck wants asked, measure the answers precisely, and do the math correctly, you just don't get the results that Dweck says you do. The numbers don't add up.

In chapters 1 through 3, we looked at dozens of psychology and neuroscience studies that support Dweck's hypothesis. Each one of the arrows in figure 3.1 has several studies to support it.

At the same time, psychologists have done other versions of those studies and gotten different results. Researchers call these studies "non-replications." When researchers tried to replicate Dweck's results, their data didn't lead to statistically significant findings.

Non-replication is a big deal. Science depends on replication. If I create a drug that truly reduces blood pressure, that drug should work not just in one study but in (almost) all of them. If mindset theory is true, then well-designed research should get positive results quite consistently. The more non-replications we get, the more worried we should be.

When researchers get competing results, they often create a grand equation comparing results from many different studies. This technique—called meta-analysis—might clarify this muddle. Rather than a back-and-forth shouting match—"This study shows that mindsets matter!" "Well, *this* study shows *they don't*!"—a meta-analysis can aggregate the data and come up with a unified answer.

Because of their potential analytical power, a recent mindset meta-analysis caused quite a stir. Researchers at Case Western Reserve University and Michigan State University looked at more than three hundred mindset studies that included more than four hundred thousand participants (Sisk, Burgoyne, Sun, Butler, & Macnamara, 2018). The conclusion: mindsets have a measurable but small effect on academic achievement. And the strategies used to promote GM don't help that much.

This meta-analysis prompted Nick Soderstrom's concern that mindset theory might be the new learning styles. It might cause you to have the same worry.

BEYOND CRISIS TO CONFIDENCE

Despite these sincere and plausible doubts, we do have good reason to believe mindset theory and to use the strategies discussed above. Four considerations give us meaningful confidence.

First, that big meta-analysis energized a lot of headlines but isn't the last word on the subject. Other people have looked at large populations and found impressive effects.

As we saw in chapter 3, Claro and Loeb studied data on more than 125,000 students in California (2017). They found that mindsets matter a lot. Using one kind of calculation, they determined that—in effect—GM-fueled intrinsic motivation gave students an extra twenty days of learning. (Because this study was published by the Brookings Institution and not by an academic journal, it wasn't included in the 2018 meta-analysis.)

Also, the skeptical 2018 meta-analysis must face off against an upbeat meta-analysis looking at mindsets and goals. This 2013 meta-analysis concluded—as the title crisply says—"mindsets matter" (Burnette, O'Boyle, VanEpps, Pollack, & Finkel, 2013). One meta-analysis might seem to answer the question for good, but conflicting meta-analyses muddle our certainty.

When considering the value of meta-analysis, by the way, we should also note that many insightful scholars harbor deep skepticism about this technique. One objection can be summed up quite easily: "garbage in, garbage out." If the meta-analysis includes faulty studies or excludes useful ones, then its validity suffers. The decision to exclude the Brookings Institution study from the 2018 meta-analysis makes sense according to its stated criteria. But that's a huge data pool to set aside, especially when it was created by such a widely respected organization.

In brief: meta-analysis gives us one way to explore mindset theory. But even if we accept meta-analysis as a technique—and not everyone does—we've got conflicting meta-analyses, as well as other very large data sets.

Second, we should ask not simply, "Do mindset interventions work?" but "Do they work compared to something else?"

This series of books considers several pools of neuroscience and psychology research that helps classroom teachers. The first book, *Learning Begins*, looked at working memory and attention. The third book, *Learning Thrives*, will explore research into long-term memory: encoding, consolidation, and retrieval. The book you're reading focuses specifically on motivation.

Sadly, psychologists struggle to develop theories of motivation that provide useful teaching advice. As we saw in the introduction, even the American Psychological Association admits this lamentable truth: "Educationally relevant conceptions of motivation have been elusive" (Editorial, 1986, p. 1040).

Even if the 2018 meta-analysis is true, even if mindset theory has only a small influence on motivation, the fact that it has *any* influence on motivation makes it worth our interest and attention.

True enough, research into working memory and attention and long-term memory provides other strategies, many of which have greater power to influence our students' learning. And yet, as long as schools teach material that isn't intrinsically interesting to all students, teachers will want some way to think about motivation. Mindset theory offers the best approach we have.

Third, we saw in chapter 3 that mindset theory has support not only in psychology but also in neuroscience. To non-scientists, this distinction might seem unimpressive. Because both sciences focus on brains, we might assume that they always lead to the same results. However, the fields themselves differ profoundly. For much of the twentieth century, they eyed each other from a wary distance. Psychologists, in particular, discouraged one another from relying on the "black box" known as the physical brain.

The additional support provided by neuroscience, in other words, really matters. Two very different kinds of scientific inquiry point in the same direction. It would be, technically speaking, "weird" for two such different disciplines to arrive at the same wrong conclusion.

The fourth reason to find mindset theory persuasive is the most personal of the bunch.

To write this book, I spent more than ten months reviewing the history of mindset research. I've read literally dozens of research studies going back more than four decades. These studies follow an exacting formula. Each one asks a narrow question, proposes a precise hypothesis, explains its methodology in (often soporific) detail, and reports its numerical findings.

When reading these studies, we don't have to accept the authors' conclusions. We can, instead, unearth flaws in the research methodology or conclude that the statistical findings don't truly support the authors' hypothesis. We don't have to take their word for it; we can decide for ourselves.

For example: this book does not cite one of the most-quoted studies in the field because I think its methodology is flawed. In my opinion, the researchers asked leading questions. Other people apparently find that study persuasive. I just don't.

This lengthy investigation has revealed researchers' remarkable diligence, precision, and thoughtfulness. Mindset theory did not appear like magic in 2006 when Dweck published her well-known book. Instead, she and dozens of other scholars assembled it question by question, study by study, rejoinder by rejoinder.

Unlike some other researchers, Dweck listens to critics with an open mind. For instance, some scholars (e.g., Elliot, 1999) critiqued her work on performance goals and learning goals. Rather than ignore or downplay this critique, she revised her research paradigms and made her theory more precise (Grant & Dweck, 2003). Dweck did not get defensive or claim that people misunderstand her or hide behind statistical models. She updated her theory.

Simply put: Dweck does not discount her critics; she engages them. As a result, mindset theory has grown and changed over the years.

To be clear, I do have some criticisms of Dweck's work. Specifically, she cites unpublished research more often than most psychologists do. One review article cites four unpublished studies on one page alone (Dweck & Leggett, 1988). That unpublished research might hold up on inspection. However, because we can't inspect it, we have no way to assess its validity.

And yet, despite this frustration, I find the cumulative weight of mindset research deeply compelling. Each piece of figures 3.1 and 3.4 has several studies behind it. Each study carefully distinguishes between one set of possible responses (those that would refute a hypothesis) and another (which would confirm it). Unless dozens of people have been remarkably clumsy (or consistently dishonest), the grain-by-grain logical assembly makes the whole much more persuasive than the sum of its parts.

In fact, mindset research continues—and continues to find positive results. Just weeks before this book went to the publisher, two researchers explored the relationship between mindset and "intellectual humility"; that is, the willingness to believe that I'm wrong and that you might have something to teach me (Porter & Schumann, 2018). As they predicted, prompting students to adopt a growth mindset made it likelier that they would admit not knowing something. GMs made them likelier to compliment others on their intellectual strengths. Students with a GM sought out critical feedback more often. They worried less when others pointed out their mistakes. In brief: a GM promoted intellectual humility.

Of course, it would be odd for a GM to have that effect if GMs don't really exist.

Like Dweck, I trust in the scientific method and will follow its conclusions. If at some point, the weight of evidence tips against mindset theory, I'll stop advocating for it. I have little doubt that Dweck would do so too. For today, I do think teachers have four decades of reasons to trust in Dweck's ideas, methods, and conclusions. To boost intrinsic motivation, we can help students along the path that starts with a growth mindset.

MINDSET FAQS

When I talk with teachers about mindsets, these questions come up most frequently:

1. So, are you saying everyone's equally smart? If we all just have the right mindset, we'll all win Nobel Prizes?

I have heard some people extrapolate Dweck's ideas to this extreme, but I don't believe that, and Dweck doesn't either (2006).

As Blackwell writes: "Believing intelligence to be malleable does not imply that everyone has exactly the same potential in every domain, or will learn everything with equal ease. Rather, it means that for any given individual, intellectual ability can always be further developed" (Blackwell et al., 2007, p. 247).

Each of us has relative strengths and weaknesses. I'm not very good at making music (ten years of piano lessons highlight this truth), but I'm unusually comfortable speaking in front of large crowds. People are different, and—crucially—*it is not dangerously FM of me to acknowledge that truth*.

However, it would be FM to believe that we can never change. I plan to take up the piano again when I retire. This time, I will approach its challenges with a GM. I expect I'll make a lot more progress than I did before.

In the same way, if you are not comfortable speaking in front of large crowds, you can admit that truth without being guilty of FM crimes. As long as you acknowledge that you could get better at public speaking if you set your mind to it, you're well within GM territory.

2. Do students have different mindsets in different subjects? That is: could a student be GM in biology class and FM in language arts?

We have very little research that answers this precise question. Working with third through sixth graders, Stipek and Gralinski anticipated that grade school children would have different mindsets in math and social studies but found the opposite: "there was . . . no support for the hypothesis that elementary school age children have subject-specific beliefs about ability and performance" (Stipek & Gralinski, 1996, p. 403).

Researchers have found distinct mindsets about broad categories of human ability. For instance, I might have a FM about my *academic ability* but a modest GM about my *ability to make friends* and a strong GM about my *ability to improve at basketball* (Dweck, Chiu, & Hong, 1995; Erdley, Loomis, Cain, Dumas-Hines, & Dweck, 1997; Sarrazin, Biddle, Famose, Cury, Fox, & Durand, 1996).

I strongly suspect that students can have subject-specific mindsets based on their teacher's behavior. If we work and talk with our students appropriately, we can inculcate a GM: at least in our classroom, at least for this one year.

3. Where does Angela Duckworth's "grit" fit in your model?

Psychological models don't always fit tidily together. In this case, "grit" is probably an easy way to describe the *charge!* response in step 4. Gritty students charge; gritless ones retreat.

4. In Learning Begins*, you argued that working memory can't be artificially increased. Isn't that a fixed mindset? Won't my working memory increase if I have a growth mindset about it?*

I'm 5'10" and therefore rarely a first choice for pickup basketball games.

I might say to myself: "I can get better at basketball only if I get taller, and I can't get taller, so I give up." That's a fixed mindset.

I might instead say: "I might be only 5'10", but if I study tapes of Muggsy Bogues, I might learn several new ways to use my relative brevity to my advantage. Of course, I'll have to practice this new approach ferociously . . ." Now I've entered the world of growth mindset.

The same lesson holds true for working memory (WM).

We just don't have much good research suggesting that WM can be increased. And, we have no reason to believe that a growth mindset will change that result—for the same reason that a growth mindset won't make me taller: working memory and height simply can't be artificially changed (*yet*).

However, I can get better at *using the working memory I have*, in the same way I can get better at basketball using the height I have.

Learning Begins argues that, since we can't artificially increase working memory, we have to be strategic in using the capacity we have. Likewise, we have to be strategic in helping our students use theirs. If we and they use better strategies, our students will learn more. That's as growth mindset as it gets.

5. There's been a lot of talk about failure. What about success? Do FM and GM students think differently about their accomplishments?

Yes, indeed.

When a FM student faces a setback, she typically sees the setback as a confirmation of her mindset: "I knew that people have unchangeable limits on their intelligence, and my failure here shows where my own limit is."

Failure tells her something meaningful about herself and about her theory of intelligence.

However, when a GM student faces a setback, she typically doesn't perceive it as a setback. Instead, it's a useful data point, a sign saying, "I need to work harder on this part right here." For GM students, failure doesn't really register as failure.

When a GM student *succeeds*, she typically sees that success as a confirmation of her mindset: "I knew that I could do it if I worked hard enough. And: *voila!*" Success tells her something meaningful about herself and about her theory of intelligence.

Dweck & Co. use the word "diagnostic" to make this point. FM students think of failure as "diagnostic": the moment of failure diagnoses the limits of their intelligence. GM students think of success as "diagnostic": accomplishment diagnoses the limitlessness of their intelligence (Diener & Dweck, 1980).

6. What about an optimistic *mindset? Or an* international *mindset?*

Given the popularity of mindset theory, many people have taken the word "mindset" and stapled it to their own, unrelated theory. Just because someone calls their work "XYZ mindset" doesn't mean that the theory has anything to do with mindset theory. Nor does it necessarily have any research support behind it.

In short, when someone speaks glibly about some new mindset ("technology mindset," "collaboration mindset"), ask to see some research before you start listening.

7. Are there age limits? At some point, are students too young or old for mindsets to matter?

The short answer: no. We have good research showing the effect of mindset on children in pre-K (Smiley & Dweck, 1994) and on adult learners (Martocchio, 1994).

8. Much of the research you cite comes from the United States. What about other countries? Are there cultural differences?

Almost all psychology research takes place in North America and Europe (Henrich, Heine, & Norenzayan, 2010). For that reason, this question can't be answered with certainty.

A few studies suggest that Eastern cultures—Japan and Taiwan—generally promote GM whereas Western societies—the United States and Canada—promote FM (Heine et al., 2001; Nisbett, 2003; Stevenson, Chen, & Lee, 1993).

While this formulation may be useful in some settings, we shouldn't rely on it too heavily. "Eastern" and "Western" are dramatic oversimplifications (derived, of course, by "Westerners"). We need much more research about the specific differences among the dozens of cultures that make up these groups before we say anything with much certainty.

For example, in the fall of 2016, I discussed mindset research at the African Leadership Academy, a school in Johannesburg, South Africa. ALA draws students and teachers from across the African continent, and so I grabbed my chance to do a little informal research. I asked: are there mindset variations across African regions?

As you can imagine, these questions provoked a thoughtful and energetic debate. As far as ALA teachers could tell, there are specific mindset differences among cultures: some lean this way; others lean another. But no one identified a clear pattern that tidily divides Africa into FM and GM zones.

Of course, MBE principle #3 reminds us: averages matter for groups but not individuals. It *may* be true that students in the United States are more prone to a FM than students in Japan, but that potential truth does not mean anything about this one student sitting in front of me right now.

9. I've tried to look at some of the research you cite, but the terminology is quite different. What's going on?

In the field of psychology, any one concept can have several different names. (We shouldn't point fingers. The same can be true in neuroscience and education research.)

Mindset research suffers from this problem. The step-4 response that I call "charge" is often referred to as a "mastery response." Sadly, the step-2 goal here described as a "learning goal" is often called a "mastery goal." Other scholars have conflicting names for the steps described here.

If you think you're starting to feel confused, don't worry—it gets worse. When Dweck initially developed her theories, she used much clunkier language.

People who think that intelligence can't change think of it as *one thing*; that is, they think of it as an *entity*; that is, they are "entity theorists."

People who think that intelligence can change think of it *accumulating small new pieces*; that is, they think of it as *incrementally malleable*; that is, they are "incremental theorists."

So people with a fixed mindset are "entity theorists"; people with a growth mindset are "incremental theorists." (You've seen this terminology in Blackwell's first graph: figure 3.2.)

There is no polite way to say this: these terms are awkward, cumbersome, and anti-intuitive. I myself believe that *Mindset* has sold so well because the phrases "fixed and growth mindset" are so helpfully intuitive. Dweck's book may be the most effective rebranding in the history of psychology.

In fact, the four-step framework presented here grew out of my own schematic attempts to keep all the terminology straight. By making enough lists and drawing enough arrows, I could sort out how all the research pieces fit together. To make sense of the research yourself, I suggest you keep coming back to figures 3.1 and 3.4. Whatever *terms* the researchers use, the *concepts* should be quite clear. You'll know then which piece of the mindset puzzle is being investigated.

10. I have to say, I'm skeptical about Dweck's questionnaires. Can you really learn about an important part of someone's psyche by having them rate answers to a question on a scale of 1–7?

It's always appropriate to be skeptical about scientific research. Science, after all, is a way to organize skepticism.

We can start to answer this question in two ways.

First, Dweck and her colleagues are quite open about their methodology in asking questions and analyzing the answers. If you want all the details about their mathematical models, check out pages 269–273 of Dweck, Chiu, and Hong's article (1995). Clearly, mindset researchers have scrupulously ensured that their analysis meets all the statistical requirements that we could want.

Second, if the statistics answer isn't persuasive, then perhaps the *grade* research and *neuroscience* research in chapter 3 will be. If Dweck's questionnaires aren't getting at real differences in human motivation, then it's very puzzling how well and how often they predict students' academic accomplishment. And it's equally puzzling that we see different neural behaviors for FM and GM thinking.

11. When I look at some of the studies, I see your descriptions don't include everything. Why do you leave out chunks of Dweck's work?

(A) I'm glad you're looking up those sources; that's why I cite so many of them. If you find yourself struggling to make sense of them, maintain a growth mindset and keep going. You'll get used to the terminology and the research paradigms if you push through the confusion and read as many as you can.

(B) Because the mindset research is so complicated, I've tried to keep my descriptions as direct and simple as possible. At times, especially in the early chapters, the desire for simplicity means I leave out some of the subtopics that Dweck explores.

(C) I have, in fact, deliberately changed one detail in a description of Dweck's work with Diener (1978). You may recall the student who kept guessing "star" because he liked constellations. In reality, the student kept guessing "brown" because he liked chocolate. However, because this book doesn't include color prints, that detail wouldn't make much sense. I switched to "star" and "constellations" to make the point as clear as possible.

12. I have another concern about these studies. It seems that Dweck spent a lot of time making kids feel dumb. How is this ethical?

Dweck shares your concern and was very careful to ensure that students came away from these studies feeling successful and well-informed.

In studies with younger students, for example, she typically told participants that the difficult problems had been designed for students who were older than they. In fact, she continued, they had a chance to solve those difficult puzzles only because they had done so well on the earlier ones (Mueller & Dweck, 1998). Dweck is emphatic on this point: she worked hard to be sure that students left these studies feeling happy and proud.

With college students, her team always explained the research paradigms to participants after the study was over. For example, Hong's study initially gave students fake articles showing that 88 percent of intelligence comes either from genes or from the environment (Hong et al., 1999). At the conclusion of the study, students were given both articles, told that both viewpoints are prevalent, and given sources to read to learn more about this debate.

13. Wait, is the brain really like a muscle?

The brain is a fantastically complex beast. The metaphors we use to describe it can clarify its function in some ways but mislead in others.

You might have heard that the prefrontal cortex is the "conductor" of the brain. Or that stress "bruises" the amygdala. Both of those comparisons help us understand key concepts by drawing on prior knowledge. But they're also wrong in a great many ways. The prefrontal cortex, for example, never wears tails.

When we say that "the brain is like a muscle," we want students to recognize that practice can improve function, just as exercise can improve strength. Of course, brains don't get physically bigger when we learn new things. In this way and many others, the analogy is useful but not literally true.

14. Aren't racism and sexism, in effect, pathologically fixed mindsets? Why haven't you said anything about them?

Indeed they are.

This topic is so important, and the answers so fascinating, that they get their own chapters. Keep reading.

Part II

STEREOTYPE THREAT

Chapter Five

(De)Motivation and Stereotypes

Imagine this strange day in your classroom. Preparing to teach a particular topic—say, basic comma rules—you give your two sections a pretest. Both groups average 70 percent. You then discuss comma usage and give your students several practice problems. When you quiz them the next day, your first class averages 77 percent. A ten percent improvement in one day suggests real teaching chops. Perhaps you allow yourself a celebratory extra cup of coffee.

To your dismay, however, the second class's quiz average *drops to 67 percent*. Looking at these results, pouring that coffee down the sink, you wonder what on earth has led to such starkly different outcomes. The two classes, once exactly matched, now differ by a full letter grade.

Sian Beilock had just such a puzzling day in her psychology lab. She invited several golfers to undertake a simple task: putt from nine different locations on a putting green and be as accurate as possible (Beilock, Jellison, Rydell, McConnell, & Carr, 2006). These men, chosen for their love of the game and their low handicap, may well have thought the assignment a gimme.

When they studied the green, however, those golfers realized the task was harder than it sounded. At the center of the green, Beilock had placed not a *cup* but a small, flat *target*. The golfers thus faced an unusual challenge. If they struck the golf ball too firmly, it would roll over and past the target, not fall into a cup. As they contemplated their putts, they doubtless subtly backed off their stroke to avoid overhitting the ball.

After the first round of putts, the golfers read a short passage about the purpose of Beilock's study: ostensibly to understand "individual differences in golf putting performance" (Beilock et al., 2006, p. 1064).

They then repeated their putts. When the researchers compared the second round of putts to the first, they found that these golfers—like your first section—improved 10 percent. With practice, they got better.

Beilock's team then invited a second group of golfers to repeat these three steps: several putts, reading a short passage about the study's goal, a second round of putts. Given their expertise—again, skillful and passionate golfers—they likewise expected to improve.

Yet, in a surprising twist, they did not. They got 5 percent worse. As you see in figure 5.1, Beilock faced the same problem you just imagined in your own classroom: two groups started exactly matched, yet practice led to stark differences.

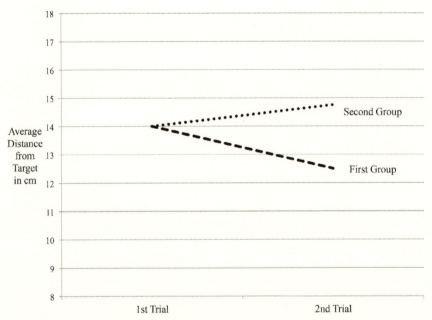

Figure 5.1. Expert Male Golfers Putting toward a Target. *Adapted from "On the Causal Mechanisms of Stereotype Threat: Can Skills That Don't Rely Heavily on Working Memory Still Be Threatened?" by S. L. Beilock, W. A. Jellison, R. J. Rydell, A. R. McConnell, & T. H. Carr, 2006, Personality and Social Psychology Bulletin, 32(8), p. 1064. Copyright 2006 by the Society for Personality and Social Psychology, Inc.*

This result would be surprising in your class, but it did not surprise Beilock's team. In fact, it supported the hypothesis they wanted to study. Beilock & Co. had treated these two groups slightly differently.

The short passage read by the *second* group included a few crucially different sentences. They read that "in our laboratory, we have been researching individual differences in golf putting ability and, in particular, focusing on gender" (Beilock et al., 2006, p. 1064). The passage noted that Ladies Professional Golf Association data demonstrate that *women outplay men* in the short game.

Beilock found that golf practice leads to better putting . . . unless your manly self worries that women can putt better than you.

To understand the implications of Beilock's study, we should focus on this key point: the problem was not *in the golfers* but *in the environment* in which the golfers were golfing. Beilock's team created one environment in which practice improved the golfers' scores. They just as easily created a second environment that lowered them. The golfers stayed the same. The environment shaped their success or failure.

THE SCOPE OF THE PROBLEM

Beilock's study has the advantage of being a little bit funny. You might chuckle when you think about macho athletes being thrown off their game simply by hearing about female competition. However, the topic of Beilock's study—and of part II in this book—allows few other chortles. Stereotype threat research asks us to contemplate glum topics in history and society. Happily, despite all this gloom, chapters 6 and 7 will soon give us reasons to be optimistic and strategies to be helpful.

The story of stereotype threat goes back to a young academic psychologist named Claude Steele. As his career progressed and he made his way from college to college, he investigated an unnerving pattern—one both well-researched and awkward to discuss.

High school GPA and SAT scores typically predict a student's success in college. College admission offices pay attention to those scores for this very reason. And yet Steele noticed these scores did not do such a good job predicting academic success for African American students. If researchers followed a group of white students with a particular SAT score and a group of African American students with that same SAT score, the white students would graduate with a higher average GPA than the African Americans (Steele, 2010).

Over the years, Steele developed a hypothesis to explain this puzzle, and he finally tested it when he arrived at Stanford (Steele & Aronson, 1995). He invited two groups of college sophomores to come to his psychology lab. In each group, half of the students were white, and half were black. All of the students solved problems from the verbal section of the GRE.

Steele told the first group that the problems were not a measure of their ability, and they would get helpful feedback on their work. He told the second group that the problems were "a genuine test of your verbal abilities and limitations" (Steele & Aronson, 1995, p. 799).

When the researchers described the GRE problems as "helpful practice," the black students and the white students did equally well on the test, relative to their verbal SAT scores. (The small difference isn't statistically significant.)

When they described the test as "a measure of ability," however, the black students' score fell to *half* that of the white students. Figure 5.2 can unnerve the most sanguine of teachers.

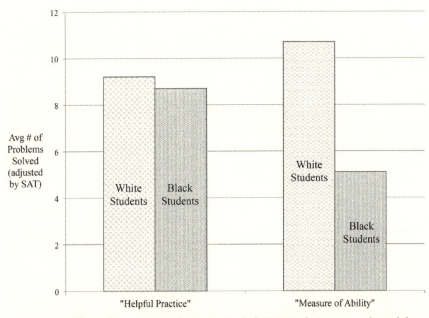

Figure 5.2. Effect of Stereotype Threat on Verbal GRE Performance. *Adapted from "Stereotype Threat and the Intellectual Test Performance of African Americans," by C. M. Steele & J. Aronson, 1995, Journal of Personality and Social Psychology, 69(5), p. 802. Copyright 1995 by the American Psychological Association.*

Note, again, the key point of Steele's research: the problem was not *in the students*. Instead, the problem was *in the environment* in which the students took the test. Steele's team created one environment in which black students' scores corresponded to those of their white peers and just as easily created another environment in which black students fell dramatically short of their white peers. Not the student but the environment was the problem.

Because these students perceived a threat that others would judge them based on stereotypes, Steele and his colleagues named this result *stereotype threat* (ST).

This first study revealed the power of stereotype threat for a specific group (African Americans) and a specific task (the verbal GRE). It also raised pressing questions. Do we find this same effect elsewhere? Does it happen for other groups? For other tests? Other abilities?

Who's Vulnerable?

Since 1995, we've learned that ST goes far beyond stereotypes about African Americans. In fact, it goes beyond racial and ethnic categories altogether. Researchers have measured the effect of ST for many kinds of identity, such as gender (Beilock, Rydell, & McConnell, 2007; Leyens, Désert, Croizet, & Darcis, 2000), sexuality (Bosson, Haymovitz, & Pinel, 2004), age (Barber & Mather, 2013), and socioeconomic status (Good, Aronson, & Inzlicht, 2003).

ST can hamper cognitive performance even for temporary identities, such as *academic major* (Croizet, Després, Gauzins, Huguet, Leyens, & Méot, 2004). In France, apparently, psychology majors face the stereotype that they just aren't as intelligent as science majors. Psych majors don't believe the stereotype, but they know it exists. Croizet & Co. followed Steele's research model and had both psych majors and science majors take a logic-puzzle test.

"Unthreatened" psych majors did just as well on those logic puzzles as their science-major peers. However, when psych majors heard that the test measured their "mathematical and logical reasoning," they fell well short of their peers. Clearly, stereotypes about short-term identities can evoke ST.

Equally important, ST can vex our ability to do almost anything: language skills, math skills, visual skills, memory skills (Johns, Schmader, & Martens, 2005; McGlone & Aronson, 2006; Smeding, Dumas, Loose, & Régner, 2013). Students under ST have greater difficulty participating in group discussions and managing inhibition (Hutchison, Smith, & Ferris 2013; Sekaquaptewa & Thompson, 2003). Even putting golf balls, as Beilock cleverly demonstrated, can be made more difficult by a relevant stereotype.

Joshua Aronson wondered if ST could muddle people who typically face *positive* stereotypes. In the United States, stereotypes often suggest that men surpass women in mathematical ability. Stereotypes likewise suggest that white students have more academic ability than other racial and ethnic groups. Considering the many stereotypes in their favor, we might plausibly think that white male math majors would shrug off ST quite effortlessly. And yet, when Aronson gathered just such a group—at Stanford, no less—they did badly on a math test *when told they were being compared to Asians* (Aronson,

Lustina, Good, Keough, Steele, & Brown, 1999). Facing stereotypes about brilliant Asian mathematicians, even these otherwise favored students wilted under pressure.

(This study calls for an important caveat. Aronson and Steele don't blame Stanford's white male math majors for the stereotypes that favor them. These students did no more to ask for positive regard than French psychology majors did to ask for doubts. For Steele and his theory, blame accrues to the *society* that fosters the stereotypes, not the *individuals* who have learned them as they grew up.)

Remarkably, ST can both impede and enhance performance—even in the same person. In the United States, as noted above, stereotypes about math ability favor men over women and Asians over whites. To study the effect of competing stereotypes, Shih, Pittinsky, and Ambady asked Asian American women to solve math problems (1999). When the researchers highlighted *gender* identity, negative stereotypes prompted lower scores. When they highlighted *racial* identity, positive stereotypes prompted higher scores.

To be thorough, Shih's team then repeated their study in Canada, where stereotypes do not link Asians with high mathematical ability. As before, when Shih focused participants on gender, math scores went down. However, when she focused their attention on racial identity, the second group saw no increase in performance. These results underline an essential conclusion: *environments shape student ability*. Performing the same study in different cultural contexts yields different results because different cultures have different stereotypes.

Steele's theory does not claim that environment determines everything. Some students do better on math tests because they know more math. To focus on the environment is not to deny this obvious truth. Instead, a focus on the environment helps us understand motivation and demotivation. The theory isn't trying to make excuses; it's trying to solve practical problems.

Stereotype Threat Meets fMRI

As in part I, teachers might find this psychology research more persuasive were it backed by neuroscience. If ST really exists—and does not result from sloppy research and wishful thinking—then we should expect predictable differences in brain function.

Specifically, when math students *do not face* ST, we would expect more effective processing in brain regions associated with math. When they *do face* ST, we would anticipate less effective processing in those brain regions and more activity in brain regions associated with emotional threat.

In an fMRI study, Anne Krendl found exactly this pattern. She asked women to solve math problems and subjected half of them to ST (Krendl,

Richeson, Kelley, & Heatherton, 2008). When she monitored brain activity during this process, she detected these recognizable and predictable patterns. Brain regions integral to mathematical processing (the angular gyrus, the left parietal cortex, and the prefrontal cortex) showed measurably more activity for the non-stereotype-threat group, whereas regions that process emotional threats (the lower portion of the anterior cingulate cortex) showed greater activity among threatened students.

As is true for any fMRI study, the technical details can be overwhelming. (If you'd like to learn more about specific Regions of Interest—especially the left superior temporal gyrus—be sure to read the fine print of Krendl's study.) But as in part I, a neuroscientific approach does help validate the psychology research. In brief: brains under ST behave differently, and predictably differently, from unthreatened brains.

Krendl's findings about ST might remind us of Mangels's findings about mindset. They should also remind us of relevant caveats. We can easily misinterpret brain research to suggest that some people are "hardwired" to experience ST. However, we know that practically anyone (white men, Asian women) can experience ST in their attempts to do practically anything (putt golf balls, solve math problems).

Like "mindset," "stereotype threat" does not describe a kind of person. Instead, it describes responses to specific conditions. When I think about playing the piano, I have a strongly fixed mindset; I just can't do it. When I think about public speaking, I have a strongly growth mindset; I'm confident I can get better.

In a similar way, when I learned in school that left-handedness has—at certain historical times—been associated with immorality, that stereotype had no influence on me. I'm right handed, so I didn't respond strongly to that information. However, if I grew up in a society that stereotypes blue-eyed people—perhaps everyone thinks they are naturally clumsy—then I might experience ST. After all, I am a blue-eyed klutz.

A fixed mindset and a ST response don't make up enduring parts of my personality. They occur when specific circumstances flummox my motivation in precise ways.

Conversations about stereotypes, especially racial stereotypes, can make us deeply uncomfortable. Because of historical inequalities in the United States—in particular, the history of excluding people of color and women from educational opportunities—such conversations can prompt anger, shame, and defensiveness. And yet, as we will see, Steele's research explicitly rejects blame and finger-pointing. Instead, he guides us to a more hopeful perspective. If some students struggle relative to their peers because of the environment, we have cause for optimism. Because *teachers can change the environment*.

MAPPING STEREOTYPE THREAT PARADOXES

The introduction spoke enthusiastically about the benefits of counterintuitive research findings. Teachers learn most from science that gives us new ideas, not from research that simply confirms what we've always been doing.

However, ST research strains that principle nearly to the breaking point. As psychologists have explored ST, they have uncovered unexpected finding upon unexpected finding. As they accumulate, we can struggle to make sense of them all. These psychological reverses can pose real problems because they might lead teachers astray.

That is, we teachers are a practical people. When we learn about ST, we immediately start looking for solutions. Yet unless we know how and why ST operates as it does, our solutions might not fix the problem. They might even exacerbate the problem. For that reason, before we start seizing on solutions, we should understand the psychological mechanisms that produce ST. This deeper understanding allows us to heal the ill that Steele has diagnosed.

ST begins with four preconditions. If students experience all four, they most likely respond in three ways. Those three responses, in turn, doubly interfere with effective cognition. This causal chain—*preconditions* lead to *responses* that hamper *thinking and concentration*—creates the ST effect. Once we understand this causal chain—as outlined in figure 5.3—we can prevent that process from ever getting started.

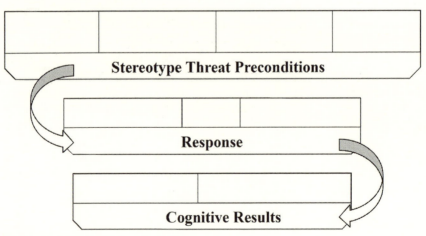

Figure 5.3. Stereotype Threat Outline

Preconditions

Over the past twenty years, researchers have identified four preconditions that lead to ST. If the environment includes all four, then the student facing them will—most likely—learn less, do badly on tests, and emotionally withdraw from the school, the discipline, or the topic (Appel & Kronberger, 2012).

Precondition #1: Salience

Imagine a society with the stereotype that *good swimmers just don't learn foreign languages very well*. If a student named Cody—star of his school's swimming team—sees a poster depicting Michael Phelps in his Spanish classroom, his thoughts suddenly turn to his own swimming career. Before class started, Cody gave no thought to the pool. Now he can't stop thinking about it ... and about the well-known relationship between swimming success and language learning.

In the vocabulary of psychology, Cody's swimming skill is now "salient" to him. He consciously considers himself as member of the category "swimmer." Stereotype threat doesn't take place without salience. Unless Cody recognizes that a part of his identity faces a relevant stereotype, ST won't hamper his Spanish performance.

Sadly, even subtle cues make parts of our identity salient. When students fill out demographic information before standardized tests, for example, they typically indicate gender, race, and parental education. Simply filling out that information makes these identities salient to test takers and thus can prompt ST. For example, if African American students take a math test, they do better if they indicate their race *after* the test rather than *before* it—because simply checking a box has made their race salient (Alter, Aronson, Darley, Rodriguez, & Ruble, 2010).

Over the past twenty years, researchers have routinely found how depressingly easily they can make stereotypeable identity salient. Women in STEM disciplines can experience ST when alone in a group of men. Their solitude makes their identity salient (Sekaquaptewa & Thompson, 2003). This effect takes place even when they merely see a video of women outnumbered by men at a STEM conference (Murphy, Steele, & Gross, 2007).

Were Cody the only swimmer in his Spanish class, then the poster of Michael Phelps might be all the more disruptive.

Precondition #2: Secondhand belief

Renowned debater Lucy lives in a society where *debaters are thought to be bad at grammar*. When her English teacher praises the Lincoln-Douglas debates, Lucy abruptly starts thinking about her own forensic prowess—and recalls the stereotype about her passion.

Yet free-thinking Lucy doesn't accept her culture's stereotype. From her point of view, this belief just makes no sense, and she knows quite confidently that she can learn grammar as well as anyone.

Will her teacher's admiration for Honest Abe affect Lucy's performance on the upcoming grammar test? Does ST muddle people who don't believe the underlying stereotype?

Sadly, yes. In fact, the news gets worse. ST will hamper Lucy's performance even if her teacher and her classmates reject this belief. Remarkably, *no one in the room* needs to believe a stereotype for ST to work.

However, if Lucy *believes that her teacher believes* the stereotype, this "secondhand belief" can trigger ST. Lucy might have it all wrong. The teacher might have done grad school research on the grammar prowess of famous debaters. And yet, even Lucy's inaccurate beliefs about her teacher can trigger this effect.

As Steele emphasizes in *Whistling Vivaldi*, this precondition seems bizarre. It means that ST can happen "without bad intentions, without the agency of prejudiced people" (Steele, 2010, p. 42). As noted above, Steele does not point fingers in blame. He focuses on the effect that stereotypes have within a society at large, not on an individual's "bad intentions" or "the agency of prejudiced people."

How do researchers know that such secondhand beliefs can trigger ST? You recall Beilock's golfers staring at that strange putting green. When Beilock informed the second group that women putt more skillfully than men, those golfers did not believe her. In fact, *no stereotype holds that women putt better than men*. The researchers invented this claim. Although the golfers themselves did not believe the stereotype, they did believe that *Beilock's research team* believed it. Their secondhand belief—"I believe that you believe"—triggered the ST effect.

This precondition leads to two strange, even unnerving, implications. First, teachers can trigger ST for stereotypes we've never heard of and know nothing about.

When, for example, students come to our classrooms from other countries and cultural backgrounds, they may well bring with them their own stereotypes. Perhaps in some countries, green-eyed people are believed to be especially bad at fractions. As a math teacher, I may never have heard of this stereotype and certainly don't believe it. However, my own disbelief does not dispel the danger. My student's secondhand belief—he believes that I believe—creates a problem I don't even suspect exists.

The second implication of precondition #2 takes on a moral dimension. Everyone reading this sentence grew up in a culture cluttered with stereotypes about race, class, gender, sexuality, religion, handedness, weight, hair color, and so forth. Immersed in such stereotypes, we most certainly came to believe some of them—at least in part. In the same way we simply absorbed our native languages, we absorbed the prejudices that those native languages sometimes express.

Knowing that such stereotypes harm our students and our society, many teachers strive to change our schools and our own minds. And yet, if the research quoted here is true, then we should both pursue this course *and do even more*. If secondhand beliefs can trigger ST, then it isn't enough for us to rid ourselves of stereotypes. After all, to quote Steele again, ST can happen "without bad intentions, without the agency of prejudiced people." Even if, by some miraculous process, we rid ourselves completely of stereotyped beliefs, ST might nonetheless trouble our students' learning. After all, they—like Lucy—might not know their teacher's true state of mind.

This weighty task may indeed feel daunting. Rest assured: practical solutions are coming soon. The more we understand ST, the more skillfully we can defuse it.

Precondition #3: Skill and Interest

Kaylee's family has moved to a country where folk wisdom holds that *gymnasts never master geometry*. In math class, her friends' gentle teasing about her balance bar routine keeps this stereotype salient (precondition #1) and causes Kaylee to believe that others believe (precondition #2).

Intrepid Kaylee, however, has always rocked math. She mastered multiplication facts well before her peers, works all the bonus problems in each chapter, and does Kendoku puzzles for fun.

For all these reasons, Kaylee's teacher doesn't fret. Given her obvious math accomplishment and her evident delight in taking on new problems, the teacher sees no need to quell the mild teasing. Kaylee's skill and interest will, little doubt, protect her from those preconditions.

The teacher's presumption makes good sense and yet—in another counterintuitive finding—has the truth exactly backward.

Kaylee's skill at and interest in math create *special vulnerability* to stereotypes about math. Her passion and proficiency don't protect her; they imperil her.

Once again, Beilock's golfers reveal this precondition. Beilock and her team chose skilled golfers who love the game. Remember as well that Steele's first study used GRE problems with *Stanford* students: some of the best standardized-test takers in the country. A love of golf and a dexterity at parsing passages didn't provide safety from ST. They derailed performance.

Although initially surprising, this finding does make sense. Students who don't care about logic puzzles won't be influenced by a stereotype claiming that tall people stink at logic puzzles. After all, they already don't care. When researchers tested students with low math scores, the presence or absence of ST made no difference in their performance (Steele, 2010).

Precondition #4: Heavy Lifting

Varsity track athlete Brady knows the stereotype that *runners can't sing*. When his friends arrange a birthday karaoke night for him, they present him with a specially made runner's jersey. Now that his runner's identity is salient to him (precondition #1), he believes they've asked him to sing because they think he can't (precondition #2). Unbeknownst to these friends, Brady has always loved to sing with his musician grandparents and so brings both passion and practice to this challenge (precondition #3). So how will he do when "Row, Row, Row Your Boat" comes up on the karaoke screen?

Happily, after a few counterintuitive preconditions, we can go with our instincts on the fourth. As you might have predicted, ST reduces performance on *difficult* tasks but not on *easy* ones. In fact, it might improve ability slightly on simple tasks.

In this case, "Row, Row, Row Your Boat" presents few challenges to all but the most tonally challenged singer. Like everyone else, Brady has been singing RRRYB since before pre-K. He's got this one in the bag. The first three preconditions won't matter much because he's got such a light burden to carry. He'll sound like his generation's Pavarotti.

However, if the next song presents special challenges—unexpected key changes, melodic complexity, intricate lyrics—now Brady faces a steeper challenge. In addition to the first three, the fourth precondition has been met: *the work itself is hard*.

Researchers used a simple, almost funny, strategy to discover this point (Ben-Zeev, Fein, & Inzlicht, 2005). To begin with, they created the first three preconditions. Working with women who like doing math (#3), researchers had them fill out demographic information including gender (#1). (In the United States, women can always plausibly suspect that others think they're not so good at math [#2].)

With these conditions in place, Ben-Zeev's team had these women write their names in cursive several times. For the easy version of this task, the women wrote their names *forward*, as they typically would. For the difficult version, they wrote their names *backward*. If you try that yourself, the difficulty of the task will surprise you.

Ben-Zeev found that students under ST wrote their forward name *more quickly* than un-stereotyped peers. However, they wrote their backward name demonstrably *more slowly*. Simply put, ST makes *easy work easier*, while it makes *difficult work more difficult*.

Figure 5.4 summarizes the preconditions we have discussed so far.

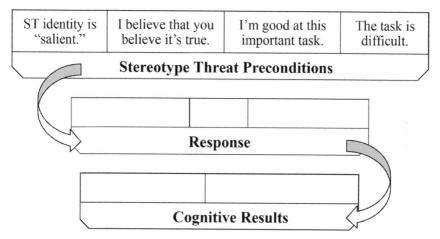

Figure 5.4. Stereotype Threat Preconditions

One important point jumps out from these final two preconditions.

When students do well in one subject, or in all of them, teachers might suggest they sign up for demanding courses or tracks: an advanced section, an AP curriculum, an honors program. It often makes sense to give passionate and successful students these extra challenges.

And yet, these challenges align all too neatly with preconditions #3 and #4. Students who enter such programs typically like and value schoolwork (#3). We routinely give them unusually difficult work (#4). We might expect advanced programs to be havens from ST. Instead, in another paradox, they might well create a perilous ST climate.

This observation, of course, does not forbid schools from offering such programs. After all, they may well be exactly what schools, students, and families need most. On the other hand, they may be fertile soil for ST seeds (Steele, 2010). Knowing the paradoxical preconditions of ST, teachers in honors programs and AP sections should keep a sharp eye out for the symptoms. And we should proactively exercise the anti-ST strategies outlined in chapters 6 and 7.

Ineffective Responses

Stereotype threat, then, results from four preconditions:

1. The stereotypeable part of my identity is *salient*.
2. I *believe (perhaps erroneously) that others believe* the stereotype.
3. I *enjoy* and *excel in* a particular discipline.
4. I'm undertaking *difficult work*.

The next gear in the ST machine seems obvious enough: these preconditions turn into a self-fulfilling prophecy. When Cody contemplates the forces aligned against him, he will collapse into a pile of chlorinated despair. "Everyone thinks swimmers can't learn Spanish," Cody will think to himself, "and they must be right. I can't do it. I give up."

Here again, as happens so often in ST research, this obvious hypothesis reverses the truth. Students facing ST do not collapse into helplessness. Precondition #3 explains why.

Remember that ST particularly affects students who love a discipline and who excel at it. For this reason, they don't give up—they *fight back*. Yet in a terrible irony, this determination to fight back leads them badly astray. It prompts highly ineffective thought patterns and behaviors. These very thoughts and behaviors, intended to disprove the stereotype, distract the student and undermine cognitive performance.

In other words: when Lucy sees a difficult grammar problem, she does not think, "Debaters never master subordinate clauses!" and start weeping. She does not give up. Instead, she grits her teeth and—quite admirably—determines to show her friends how wrong they are. And yet, her laudable efforts to fight back get in her way.

Since Steele's initial study, researchers have found three particular "fight back" responses that impede student learning.

Fighting Back Part 1: Internal Vigilance

Feisty Lucy wants to prove her doubters wrong. Because everyone believes that debate folk can't understand grammar, she is determined to ace this test. An A+ will be her best revenge.

The first question on the test asks her to identify the parts of speech in this sentence: "The poodle ate the umbrella." Lucy's mental dialogue sounds like this:

"Poodle" is obviously a noun.
"Ate" is obviously . . .
Wait just a minute.
Is "poodle" really a noun? Okay, back up: a noun is "a person, place, thing, or idea."
But a poodle isn't a *person*. And it's not a *place*. And it's not a *thing*. (My grandmother would kill me if I called a poodle a *thing*.) And it's certainly not an *idea*. So I guess a poodle *isn't* a noun.
Maybe it's an adjective?
Okay, back up. Adjectives answer the questions: How many? What kind of? Which one?
So is the word "poodle" answering the "how many?" question . . .

As you can see, Lucy's thinking has gone off the rails here: "poodle" obviously fits the definition for noun. (A poodle is a *thing* that has the *idea* it's a *person*.) Note that the problem here results not from Lucy's surrender but from her stubbornness. All this time wasted scrutinizing questions that don't call for scrutiny makes her ultimate success less likely. She does not disprove the stereotype; she reinforces it.

Of course, we want our students to be careful as they work. But students can be too careful, and those facing ST often are.

Fighting Back Part 2: External Vigilance

While students facing ST monitor their own performance, they might also monitor the external world. An evolutionary psychologist would describe it this way: they might scan their environment for potential threats.

Mary Murphy tested this question with admirable straightforwardness (Murphy et al., 2007). She used a video to evoke ST for women in STEM disciplines and then asked them to write down the objects they remembered from the screening room. (She had strategically placed a portrait of Einstein, *Nature* magazine, a periodic table, and similar STEM paraphernalia throughout the room.) Sure enough, women who contemplated gender stereotypes noticed and remembered more objects than their peers who did not. In psychology speak, they were *hypervigilant*.

Varsity swimmer Cody just knows his classmates believe he'll do badly on his Spanish quiz. To prove them all wrong, he—like vigilant Lucy—takes excessive care not to make any mistakes.

He also can't help but notice what's going on around him during the quiz. Why did his teacher just look at him that way? Does she pity his inability? Why did his best friend just chuckle? Does he think Cody got question #3 wrong? Is everyone else going faster than Cody is? Is he going faster than they are?

Here again, Cody's efforts to defeat the stereotype distract and muddle his thinking.

Fighting Back Part 3: Hidden Stress

Early researchers, reasonably enough, hypothesized that stress causes much of ST's harm. After all, people who ramp up both internal and external vigilance must surely feel increased stress. We typically measure stress directly, by asking study participants to rate their stress levels. Yet during several early studies, participants consistently denied feeling such anxiety.

Jennifer Bosson and her colleagues found an indirect way to spot hidden stress: *body language* (Bosson et al., 2004). In this study, Bosson investigated the stereotype that "gay men pose a danger to young children." She had sixty or so college students, one at a time, join four- to six-year-olds at recess. The recess room had books and games and costumes, and each college student was instructed to join in a child's activities for five minutes. Crucially, sexual orientation had been made salient to half of the participants when they filled out their demographic information. (As you recall, simply having to identify their sexuality makes it—and pertinent stereotypes—salient.)

As the students joined in the children's games, Bosson had body language experts rate them on anxious behaviors: fidgeting, nail biting, stiff posture, and so on. These experts didn't even know Bosson's hypothesis, much less who was gay or straight. They simply evaluated body language.

As in earlier studies, straight and gay students rated themselves as equally not-anxious. Had Bosson stopped with self-ratings like earlier researchers, she would have concluded once again that ST does not provoke anxiety. Yet the gay students' body language revealed the anxiety that they themselves downplayed. They smiled nervously. They avoided eye contact. They played with their hair.

To be sure these experts weren't misreading ST anxiety, other researchers have measured stress physiologically. One research team tracked the blood pressure of African American men under ST (Blascovich, Spencer, Quinn, & Steele, 2001). The resulting graphs may raise your blood pressure as well.

We can even measure stress levels with sweat. When people feel even mild stress, we sweat just a tiny bit more. In an odd kind of scientific poetry, researchers call this "microsweating." When Murphy tested external vigilance in STEM women, she kept track of their pulse and their microsweating. As she suspected, these unconscious physiological measures revealed women under ST felt more stress (Murphy et al., 2007).

Why did Brady do such a bad job at his birthday karaoke? More than his un-threatened peers, he was—literally and metaphorically—*sweating*.

Figure 5.5 shows the ineffective responses that result from four preconditions.

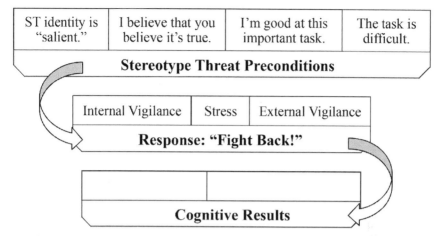

Figure 5.5. Stereotype Threat Ineffective Responses

Cognitive Difficulties

As teachers interested in psychology and neuroscience, we can recognize ST slowly accumulating its diabolical power. Four simple preconditions naturally provoke three responses. Unsurprisingly, internal and external hypervigilance—combined with stress—impede academic accomplishment. The precise cognitive mechanisms underlying this effect have gotten lots of study in recent years.

The headline: stereotype threat distracts *attention* and clutters *working memory*.

Teachers who know psychology hear *Jaws* theme music when they read that headline. In cognitive psychology, we can't do much worse than harming attention and working memory. It's a bit like hearing from your doctor: "Well, this disease is bad for your heart and your brain." If those two essentials are endangered, then the skin rash that had been bothering you doesn't seem like such a big deal anymore. You've got much bigger problems.

Attention

As teachers, we understand exactly why attention matters so much. At almost every second, we want our students to focus *here* and not to focus *anywhere else*. If ST interferes with attention, it obviously makes learning much more difficult.

In fact, the golfers we met at the beginning of the chapter demonstrate the dangers ST poses to this critical mental faculty. In brief: it tempts students to refocus on counterproductive places.

Like students, varsity golfers have mastered many automatic processes. They assume the correct stance, the correct grip, the correct attitude without needing to think about doing so. Those tasks take place subconsciously. However, when Beilock's male golfers heard that women putt better than they do, they started to rethink once-automatic processes. They gave conscious attention to skills that didn't need it.

We can almost hear these golfers' alarmed thought processes: "Wait, women putt better than men? Hmm. How can I change my putt to better mirror my female teammates?" They start rethinking their grip and shuffling their stance ever so slightly. This needless internal vigilance prompts them to focus attention where it shouldn't be and thereby distracts attention from its rightful place: the roll of the green, the angle of the breeze, the cut of the grass.

Our students, in the grips of ST, might find their attention similarly distracted. A student who mastered molarity months ago now stops to rethink her calculations for no good reason. A third grader, once confident in his clock-reading skills, now needs to think out loud about the difference between the short and long hands. Focusing on such basics, they don't focus on the new learning at hand.

Memory at Work

Whereas the dangers that ST poses to attention can be quickly understood, its effect on working memory requires more substantial explanation. Most teachers already know a lot about attention. Yet relatively few of us have explored working memory (WM) in much depth.

The phrase "working memory" can cause confusion because it includes the word "memory." Although WM does involve memory, we should instead focus more on the *work*. The work in working memory makes it essential for all school learning.

Imagine, for example, that I ask you to alphabetize five words: the five work days of the week. (Hint: the first one is "Monday.") Go ahead. Try to do that right now.

To accomplish this task, you went through several mental steps.

SELECT: first, you selected the relevant days of the week, Monday through Friday. Note, too, that you also selected the directions I gave you;

you could have paid attention to something else. You also had to select the order of the alphabet from your long-term memory. And, given the complexity of English, you had to select relevant spelling rules. ("Tuesday" and "Thursday" begin with the same *letter* even though they don't begin with the same *sound*.)

HOLD: having selected those four different pools of information, you had to hold on to them for a while. If at any point you forgot the directions or the order of the alphabet, then you couldn't succeed at the task.

REORGANIZE: when you selected and held successfully, you could then reorganize all those bits of information into the correct alphabetical order: Friday, Monday, Thursday, Tuesday, Wednesday.

As you can see, this mental operation did include some memory functions. You selected information in long-term memory and held it in short-term memory. Yet this task went beyond memory: you had to do mental work with all that information. That's working memory.

Here's another example: "Romeo (in Verona) and Juliet (in Padua) are 60 miles apart from each other. If Juliet skateboards toward Romeo at 15 miles per hour, and Romeo pogo-sticks toward Juliet at 5 mph, where should Friar Lawrence meet them to perform their marriage ceremony? How much time does he have to get there?"

Here again, you have to select, hold, and reorganize relevant information. How far apart are the lovers? How fast are they going? What's the appropriate mathematical formula? How do the numbers fit into that formula? Who is Friar Lawrence again? Why hasn't he been defrocked?

In addition, you need to COMBINE information to come up with new numbers. When you conclude that they'll meet up in San Bonifacio, fifteen miles outside of Verona, and that the Friar has three hours to get there, you didn't merely put numbers into a new order. You put them together in specific ways to find new numbers.

Whenever students must *select, hold, and reorganize/combine* information, they're using WM.

Of course, almost everything in school requires students to do so. When they compare two historical figures or calculate the distance a cannon can lob a ten-kilogram shell or sound out a new word, they're using WM. Even physical activities, like learning to write or dance or play the violin, require WM. Schools are shrines built to honor successful WM function.

Alas, this overview of WM has held back on a crucial fact. *We simply don't have very much WM.* Students need it for everything they do in school, but they often don't have enough to accomplish the work they've got. Working memory overload may be the most common undiagnosed problem that students encounter.

For this reason, teachers should worry when we read that stereotype threat might vex working memory. If our students always need working memory *and* they start with only a small supply *and* ST complicates working memory processes, that's a cognitive recipe for academic disaster (Watson, 2017).

Sure enough, we've got lots of research making exactly this connection. The details vary from study to study, but they typically follow a straightforward design. A research team gives students some problems that don't require working memory and similar problems that do. Students under ST do well on the easy problems. However, they stumble over harder problems. When they really need working memory, ST drains their reserves. They just don't have enough left over to solve the problems. (For example, see Beilock, Rydell, & McConnell, 2007; Hutchison, Smith, & Ferris, 2013; Schmader, Johns, & Forbes, 2008.)

"Stereotype threat harms learning by distracting student attention and cluttering working memory." That sentence sounds hyperbolically scary, as if researchers wanted to paint the glummest possible picture. Alas, no hyperbole here. ST does exactly that.

∼

In this way, several counterintuitive *preconditions* lead to several counterintuitive *responses*, which in turn upend core *cognitive functions*.

∼

As mapped in figure 5.6, seemingly small causes lead ultimately to dramatic effects.

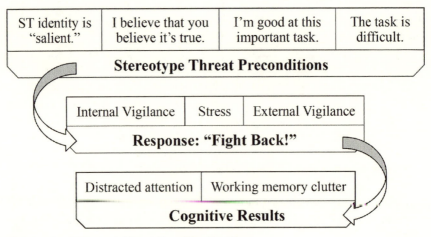

Figure 5.6. Stereotype Threat Cognitive Results

A Test Case

The model presented in figure 5.6 summarizes several dozen studies over more than two decades. It holds lots of information, densely packed into just a few boxes and arrows.

Having studied each box and each arrow on its own, we should take some time to put them all together. This exercise will help you do just that.

In 2010, Claude Steele appeared on the call-in radio show *Talk of the Nation*, hosted by Neal Conan. Early on in the program, a guest named "John" calls in to discuss his own experience with stereotypes. His story gives us a helpful chance to consider all the pieces of ST together.

When you read John's story, start by identifying the specific stereotype that troubles him. (Hint: we haven't discussed it yet.)

Then, work your way deliberately through each step of figure 5.6, asking yourself if John's story fits this model: preconditions, ineffective responses, cognitive difficulties. For example:

- Is the stereotypeable part of his identity salient to John?
- Does he believe that others believe?
- Does he seem stressed to you?
- Is his attention distracted?

In some cases, you can answer these questions by quoting John directly. In others, you might have to draw reasonable inferences. For every box, you want to know: does John's story fit the ST model, or not?

Conan: John is on the line from Manchester, New Hampshire.

John: Hey, yeah. This is John. How are you guys doing?

Conan: Good

Dr. Steele: Fine.

John: Yeah, hey. I want to say something about the [unintelligible] goes beyond, like, gender or race or class like that, but I found that since I've graduated high school, and I've yet to go to college, but I'm in the U.S. Forest Service. And so I'll show up on the worksite, and right away, they'll have this instant stigma that since I've not attended college, that they have stereotyped that I am not as qualified or capable, but it turns out I'm able to par, if not excel past their expectations. So that's one stereotype, one that maybe you guys could address for me.

Conan: Okay. As a fellow non-collegian, John, I hear you. But go ahead, Claude Steele.

John: Yeah, that's, like, that's what I'm talking about. It goes beyond, like I've seen—so I've worked with females, blacks, whites, every race you can think of, every demographic, every background. And the thing is, is like it comes down to the end of the day, you're sitting around the fire after you've just worked really hard all day in the Park Service that it'll come down to the fact that, like, they'll look at you less respectively in the one fact that you don't have that piece of paper saying you know what you know, but all the while, I've had three or four years' experience now past anything that these college graduates really have.

Like, they're all greenhorns compared to me, but since I don't have the piece of paper, there's instantly a stereotype that I don't know exactly the same, like, how to make a grade in the trail . . .

(C) 2010 National Public Radio, Inc. Excerpt from news report titled "'Whistling Vivaldi' And Beating Stereotypes" was originally broadcast on NPR's Talk of the Nation on April 12, 2010, and is used with the permission of NPR. Any unauthorized duplication is strictly prohibited.

Once you've named the relevant stereotype, take several minutes to review figure 5.6. Try not to peek at the notes below: see what you come up with on your own.

In his brief story, John identifies the stereotype that "people who haven't been to college just aren't as good at things as people who have been." Researchers have not studied this stereotype specifically. For this reason, it gives us an excellent chance to test-drive our model.

Preconditions:

1: Is John's lack of college attendance salient *to him?* Clearly yes. We know because he says so, several times.

2: Does he believe that others believe *the stereotype?* Clearly yes. He says so. (Note, by the way, that we don't know if John's belief is correct. If we asked them, John's coworkers might say they didn't even know he hadn't attended college. Or they might confirm his suspicions. All we know is that he thinks they "look at him less respectfully because he doesn't have that one piece of paper." In his experience, this stereotype kicks in "instantly.")

3: Is it important *to John to be* good *at his job?* He never says so directly. However, it certainly seems important to him. He calls Neal Conan out of concern that others think he's not.

4: Is forestry work difficult? I assume so. At the very least, we're all happy that no one hikes a trail I myself am responsible for tending.

Given that John's story meets all our preconditions, does it also suggest ineffective responses? Has his desire to disprove the stereotype led him to "fight back"?

1: Is John excessively internally vigilant? John's story doesn't answer this question directly. He's certainly competitive (he calls others "greenhorns"). This response—although not specifically provable—seems highly plausible.

2: Is John externally vigilant? Indeed. He notices how others sitting around the fire look at him after a hard day on the job. He clearly monitors their behavior quite suspiciously.

3: Is John stressed? He's stressed enough to call *Talk of the Nation* and chat with Claude Steele.

Do these ineffective responses lead John to *cognitive difficulties*?

Is his working memory *overloaded? Is his* attention *distracted?*

We can't know for sure. We can say, however, that those reactions seem quite possible. If he's hypervigilant, he might easily lose track of important trail-tending tasks. He might be so distracted by his peers' reactions that he misses key steps in his own work.

In brief, John's story has all the makings of a classic ST example. All the pieces have come together exactly as our model suggests.

John's example falls short of ST predictions in just one—albeit essential—way: *his performance doesn't suffer*. If we believe what he tells us, he hasn't gotten worse at his job because of these pressures. He tells us that he defeats his colleagues' expectations. When he calls them "greenhorns," he suggests that he's more skilled, not less skilled, than they.

Teachers often say that they doubt John's self-report. They wonder if foresters look at him less respectfully not because of a stereotype but because he didn't do a very good job that day. They point out that, even if he's better than the others, his performance might still fall short of his potential because he's muddled and distracted. Just as people under ST are often in denial about their anxiety, John might himself be in denial about his shortcomings.

Of course, we all benefit from having foresters who work at their highest capacity. If we can create a social climate where ST doesn't disorient John, he will benefit and so will we.

The next two chapters outline research-supported strategies for accomplishing exactly this mission.

URGENT STEREOTYPE THREAT FAQS

Answers to most stereotype threat FAQs will come in chapter 7. However, teachers often ask these questions with some urgency:

1. Wouldn't our students and our society benefit if we talked more about individual responsibility *than "problems in the environment"? Can we stop with the blaming of everyone else and encourage our students to look inside? Wouldn't* that *be more motivational?*

Because ST explores stereotypes and prejudices, it opens itself up to often-fierce cultural debates.

On the one hand, the Horatio Alger American dream insists that individual pluck and grit—with just a bit of good luck—can raise us from rags to riches. On the other hand, communal American dreams going back to the Puritans insist on society's role in shaping virtuous and successful individuals. That debate burns hotly in 2019, and so even a non-political presentation of ST research can evoke strong reactions.

The question, with its emphasis on personal responsibility, has at least two answers.

First, we might think of mindset theory and stereotype threat theory as complementary approaches.

Like the Horatio Alger American dream, mindset helps students contemplate their *individual* efforts and accomplishments. With a growth mindset, a student understands her own potential for improvement. She sees the importance of gritty persistence—even in the face of failure—to achieve it. With the right mental framework, cognitive rags can turn into academic riches.

Like the communal Puritan dream, ST research highlights the *social* environment that best fosters individual accomplishment. When schools and teachers use the right strategies, students no longer find themselves distracted by ST. They will be more likely to achieve their potential.

In other words, these theories work together to create both individual and communal motivational systems.

(As you may remember from chapter 4, Alfie Kohn criticizes mindset theory precisely because it highlights individual effort over communal forces. His objection, in effect, flips the FAQ above. He wants more communal American dream and less Horatio Alger. Perhaps this book will persuade you that both theories, especially in combination, can help us help our students learn.)

The second answer to this FAQ goes like this:

If the research cited here is correct, then ST in fact harms student learning. The impoverishment of their learning doesn't just harm the individual student (although it certainly does that). It doesn't just harm the group to which the stereotype attaches (although it certainly does that too). It harms all of us.

When more individuals in our society flourish, we all benefit. We get more extraordinary novels and more life-saving drugs and more technological progress and more astonishing athletic accomplishments and more healthy, productive adults to enhance our world. We get less poverty and anti-social behavior. Education really can benefit individuals and by doing so really can benefit society. Or it can fail to do those things.

The desire to reduce ST's harms might sound purely altruistic. But if the desire to right past wrongs—as they are enacted in current stereotypes—doesn't inspire you, the hope for a better world almost certainly does. That's why so many of us became teachers in the first place.

2. On a lighter note: I notice that you've been switching terminology a bit. Sometimes you say "black" and other times "African American." What's going on?

When describing a specific research study, I use the authors' language. So, Steele and Aronson (1995) say "black and white," and I follow their example when describing their work. In chapter 6, Walton and Cohen (2011) use quite different terminology: "African American and European American." I will use that language when describing their (amazing) study. When writing in my own voice, I say "African American" and "white."

3. This chapter sounds quite grim. It's like some stereotype Death Star is bearing down on Alderaan. Tell me you've got solutions.

We've got so many solutions, so many ways to disarm the ST Death Star, that we need two chapters to describe them all.

Chapter Six

Changing the Motivational Climate

When we first come across stereotype threat research, teachers often propose two seemingly obvious solutions.

1. If we want to stop ST, we should reduce the prevalence of stereotypes. As these false beliefs diminish, so too will their power to threaten our students.
2. Likewise, we can toughen students up. Stereotypes simply aren't true, and students shouldn't let themselves be so easily demotivated. If we can make our students grittier, they'll power their way past society's risible misunderstandings.

Now that we've explored the multiple counterintuitive processes by which ST operates, we can see that neither approach will accomplish its goal.

Of course, we should do everything possible to reduce stereotypes. However, precondition #2 tells us that ST results not from the stereotype itself but from one student's belief that another person holds it. I might not believe that female golfers putt better than men. If, however, male golfers believe that I do, they'll still suffer ST's consequences.

Thus, our first go-to strategy—"create a school community with no stereotypes"—*would* make society better but *wouldn't* eliminate ST. (Given human nature, it will also take a very long time.)

Alas, the "toughen-'em-up" strategy wouldn't simply be ineffective. It might even be counterproductive. Our research suggests that students don't suffer from a lack of grit. Indeed, their determination to fight back—not their inclination to give up—produces ST's problems. All that extra vigilance and stress tangle up students' cognitive systems. With their working memory askew and attention discombobulated, they can't think as clearly as their peers who feel no need to fight back.

To defeat ST, we need better strategies.

CLASSROOM STRATEGIES VS. STEREOTYPE THREAT

Chapter 5's final FAQ joked about a ST Death Star. The whole process, diagrammed in figure 5.6, seems too grim and too resilient to bring down. Facing this looming threat, what can Luke and Leia do?

In *Star Wars IV: A New Hope*, the rebel alliance finds a surprising weakness in the Death Star's plans: a small thermal exhaust port. Attacked in just the right way, that vulnerability explodes the whole system.

Researchers haven't found a way to explode ST completely. However, working like multiple Princess Leias, they have found an analogue to that small exhaust port: *salience*. Over the past twenty years, scholars have tested several strategies to *reduce the salience of stereotypeable identities*.

We can quickly see how this one "flaw in the ST Death Star" might prevent the whole system from working. If that first precondition isn't met, then the other parts simply fail to function. For example: precondition #2 says that ST takes place if "I believe that you believe." However, male golfers have no reason to think about their supposed putting inferiority if they're not thinking about gender in the first place. They therefore feel no need to disprove the stereotype—no need to "fight back"—if the stereotype isn't on their minds. They can focus all their attention on useful points because they're not distracted by useless ones.

This crucial insight—"aim for the thermal exhaust port!"—gives teachers a useful target. We can quickly identify all sorts of ways to reduce salience. And many insightful studies give us reason to trust that those strategies work.

Without salience, the Death Star is just a hard-to-steer sphere of metal floating off to the outer rim.

Addition by Subtraction (and Subtraction by Addition)

When teachers focus our efforts on reducing salience, we often propose a commonsense approach. If we identify the forces that—even unintentionally—might make stereotypes more salient, we can get rid of them. Simply put, we start reducing salience by failing to promote it in the first place.

For example: two years ago, I returned to my own high school to discuss psychology research with the faculty. Wistfully strolling familiar corridors, I spotted a photo gallery of long-serving teachers. Their portraits prompted lots of happy memories, and I regaled my guide with their endearing quirks: my French teacher's improbable love of T. S. Eliot, my physics teacher's impossibly dry humor.

My guide listened politely and then responded: "I'm so interested you're having this reaction. Other people don't see the same thing you're seeing." When I looked again, I spotted the obvious concern: every single teacher on that wall was white.

This photo gallery communicated one message to long-ago graduates: "Savor your youthful memories!" The very same photos communicated an entirely different message to current students of color: "Are you sure you really belong here?" Of course, that wasn't the goal for putting up the "rogues' gallery" in the first place. But even misty-eyed graduates have to admit that those portraits might make race and ethnicity painfully salient.

As we try our first strategy—"reducing salience by failing to promote it in the first place"—we might start by downplaying such objects and images.

When researcher Sapna Cheryan contemplated STEM stereotypes, for example, she focused on the quiet but clear messages broadcast by computer science classrooms. She hypothesized that environments can make some people feel welcome and others less so. In her phrasing, rooms might express "ambient belonging": "yes, *you* fit in here; no, *you* don't."

To better understand the "ambiance" that communicates "belonging" in the computer science world, Cheryan polled college students with a direct question: "What objects might you find in the office or dorm room of a 'stereotypical computer science geek'?" (Cheryan, Plaut, Davies, & Steele, 2009, p. 1048). The clear winner: a *Star Trek* poster. Runners up included video game boxes, junk food, and comic books. (You can admit it: your own stereotypes probably yielded similar answers.)

Cheryan's team suspected that female students seeing this kind of clutter would recall stereotypes about "computer geeks," including the belief that women can't code as well as men. Merely the stuff in the room would make their gender salient. If true, then simply replacing that stuff with non-stereotypical analogues might reduce that effect.

Following this straightforward logic, they decorated one classroom with *Star Trek* posters, Coke cans, and video games and another with nature and art posters, water bottles, and board games. They then invited men and women in to complete a survey about potential college majors.

In the stereotypical room, women expressed relatively little interest in a computer science major. In the non-stereotypical room, they showed lots. Clearly, one room unintentionally said "stay away," while the other proclaimed "all welcome here." Students know simply by walking into a classroom whether or not they belong in that field.

Clearly, stereotypical computer science rooms don't have pizza boxes and Jean-Luc Picard fan fiction in order to discourage women from belonging. However, because those objects make gender salient, they have that unintended ST effect.

This same experiment has been done with younger students as well. High school girls who predicted little interest in computer science wanted to sign right up when they saw a non-stereotypical classroom (Master, Cheryan, & Meltzoff, 2016).

We might wonder if Cheryan's solution creates a new problem. A room that encourages women to major in computer science might discourage men. The absence of Mentos cartons, the presence of waterfalls: this unfamiliar environment might unsettle computer science's main demographic. Cheryan's data, however, don't support that hypothesis. Failing to promote computer science stereotypes invites women without driving away men.

So far, we've seen that subtracting certain images from our classrooms might add to ambient belonging. We might also try the opposite approach: adding some objects to lessen a stereotype's influence.

A colleague who teaches economics has tried this approach. When he first learned about Steele's work, he quickly recognized the ST Death Star on the horizon. Although most of his economics sections enrolled boys and girls equally, his AP section rarely had more than one girl—and sometimes not even one.

He considered his classroom's "ambient belonging," hoping to welcome female students by taking down images that reinforce "guys-only" stereotypes. However, because he didn't decorate his classroom at all, he didn't see anything to take down. Whatever the economics analogue to a *Star Trek* poster would be, it wasn't there to remove.

He then reversed this approach by deliberately *putting up* images defying economics stereotypes. In Cheryan's language, he wanted his classroom ambiance to welcome all potential students. With this goal in mind, he included pictures of Janet Yellen and Raphael Bostic on his walls and reviewed his syllabus to highlight contributions by economists from many demographics.

Just as Cheryan's research supports a "take stereotypical stuff down" approach, so too Rusty McIntyre's work supports its "put counter-stereotypical stuff up" variant. Specifically, McIntyre wondered if stories of unexpected success might help (McIntyre, Paulson, & Lord, 2003).

To check this idea, he gave several women a math test. Before they took it, he had them read vignettes about unexpected successes.

One version of those vignettes starred "a group of people." For instance, in one story a "group of people" left a prestigious architecture firm to start their own. They bid against their former employer and—surprise!—won a contract to design a sculpture garden for a well-known museum.

A second version of these vignettes focused not on "a group of people" but on "Janet." That is: "Janet" left her architecture firm, won the sculpture-garden competition, and earned critical praise. These vignettes emphasized not simply that people can defy negative expectations but that women can.

Sure enough, the women who read the second group of stories outscored their peers. McIntyre's study shut down ST not by subtracting but by adding counter-stereotype stories. As Janet Yellen and Raphael Bostic look down on economics classrooms, they may welcome students to an otherwise less than fully hospitable discipline.

To make best use of this strategy, we should contemplate our particular circumstances and ask ourselves direct questions. What specific stereotypes might distract our students in our own classrooms?

Most ST research focuses on two academic stereotypes prevalent in the United States: first, the belief that racial and ethnic minorities won't learn as much as their white peers; and second, the belief that women in STEM disciplines can't perform as capably as men. If these stereotypes are relevant in our own work, then we can look for counter-stereotype examples to highlight.

- If you teach biology, perhaps Emily Rayfield's image should be on your walls. After all, she uses an engineering technique called "finite element analysis" to understand how skeletons work—and thereby how dinosaurs moved.
- If boys in your English class think that creative writing isn't manly, examples from Claude McKay or Oscar Hijuelos or Naguib Mahfouz might subtly change their minds.
- If the African American students in your school face stereotypes about mathematical ability, the book and the movie of *Hidden Figures* might help them see fresh possibilities for their academic lives.

Of course, many stereotypes exist beyond these well-researched ones. Even groups typically favored by stereotypes might be discouraged in your specific field. To take but one example: if you teach dance, the heterosexual boys at your school might think that only girls and gay men can dance. The counter-stereotypical examples you champion may help your students see past these needless limitations. (Christopher Walken dancing to Fatboy Slim, for example, helps dispel such beliefs. That man can *move*.)

We have at least one more strategy to reduce salience by failing to promote it. Lots of research suggests that African American students, for example, feel their racial identity most keenly when surrounded by white peers. A man focuses on his gender more anxiously when alone, surrounded by women.

The commonsense solution: do the best we can to ensure that no stereotyped person is "solo" in a group. If Cody has swim teammates in his Spanish class, his chlorine hair won't be so salient during vocabulary tests.

Here again, researchers have double-checked this straightforward idea. For example, Denise Sekaquaptewa had students learn unusual math procedures while being watched over a video feed (Sekaquaptewa & Thompson, 2003). The observers could be men, women, or both. Women observed by other women did better at the math than those being watched by men. Their gender simply wasn't as salient when they weren't solo.

Similarly, Nilanjana Dasgupta found that women participated in STEM discussions more freely when not a minority in the group (Dasgupta, Scircle, & Hunsinger, 2015).

This approach can guide both administrators and teachers.

When school leaders place students in sections, we can do our best to reduce "solos."

Imagine this sectioning puzzle. A high school might have two BC calculus sections and three girls enrolled in the course. If we focus on reducing *stereotypes*, we might decide to place two girls in one section and one in the other. This arrangement ensures that all boys study calculus with at least one girl and might thereby help challenge their belief that "girls can't do math."

While this solution might—in the long run—undermine *stereotypes*, it might in the short term raise the danger of *stereotype threat*. The lone girl in the second section will perceive her gender's salience all the more keenly surrounded by boys.

This conundrum calls for a careful balancing act. In an ideal world, administrators would pursue a dual strategy. First, to reduce the salience of gender and promote math learning, we would place all three female students in the same section. Second, we would ensure that the all-boys section spends plenty of time learning about female mathematicians. Even better, we should take care that this section be taught by a female teacher. This combination would, in the short term, reduce ST for the three girls and, in the long term, reduce gender stereotypes about math for the boys.

As classroom teachers, we can enact this same approach with the small groups we create. As a teacher in a majority-Asian school, I might note my white students' concern that they don't understand science as well as their peers. In this case, I would take care that lab groups in chemistry class never have just one white student in them.

We should, of course, adapt this general approach to our specific circumstances. This research strand gives us confidence that we can weaken ST by failing to make salience pertinent.

MINDSET RETURNS: THE THEORY

Many teachers quickly intuit a connection between stereotype threat and mindset, although that connection can be difficult to state precisely. At its simplest, the connection goes like this:

- A fixed mindset embraces this belief: "*We all* have a certain amount of intelligence, and that's just not going to change."
- A stereotype embraces this belief: "*Some groups* have a certain amount of intelligence, and that's just not going to change."

A stereotype, in other words, applies fixed-mindset thinking to groups and takes it to extremes.

For this reason, all the *growth mindset solutions* discussed in part I can help solve *stereotype threat problems* outlined in part II. A GM climate automatically helps reduce ST.

That conclusion sounds almost too good to be true. If, in fact, growth mindsets prevent ST, then we already have a lengthy list of solutions from part I. We've seen the research. We've considered specific classroom applications. We're already solving ST problems before we knew they—or their solutions—even existed.

As a first way to explore this connection, let's walk through one potential ST experience from a fixed-mindset perspective.

Brady knows the stereotype that runners can't sing. And, because he's the only track athlete in his school's chorus, the relevant identity is salient to him. (Brady's a bit of a contrarian, so he probably wears his team jersey to rehearsals.)

If Brady has a fixed mindset, then he starts vocal warm-ups in a difficult mental spot. With his FM perspective, he believes that people generally do have limits on various abilities. For instance, Brady knows from personal experience that some people are born runners—he's one of them. Other people—Brady's hapless uncle, for instance—wouldn't run if chased by a peckish leopard.

With such thoughts rattling about in his head, Brady might well deem it plausible that some people—say, *runners*—just can't sing. For that reason, his track jersey really matters at this moment (precondition #1). He might start to wonder if others really believe (precondition #2). He might want to stand up for himself and prove the doubters wrong ("fight back!"). This healthy determination might distract and overwhelm him. Like Alderaan, Brady's singing has been blown to smithereens.

Now, let's rewind the tape. A growth-mindset perspective takes Brady's thought process in an entirely different direction.

As he begins his vocal warm-ups, Brady might be dimly aware that some stereotype exists. His jersey might vaguely suggest its potential relevance. And yet, in this very moment, none of that much matters.

Brady knows from running that *practice matters*. Early in his track career, he used to look at his feet; now he knows to focus his gaze in the middle distance. Whereas he used to clench his fists, he now keeps his hands and wrists loose. His coach last summer taught him about abdominal breathing. As he incorporated each specific technique into his form, he got faster. Once a middle-of-the-pack runner, Brady now regularly finishes in the top ten.

With his growth mindset humming in the background, Brady trusts his experience that the right kind of work improves performance. He needn't consciously reject the stereotype about tone-deaf runners. He unconsciously knows that such limits aren't relevant to him. If he does his vocal warm-ups right, he'll sing better.

Dweck's word "diagnostic" helps explain these different thought patterns. For FM-Brady, every setback is "diagnostic" of his limits. When he misses a tricky key change in the bridge, that slip-up confirms his limits and reinforces the stereotype. For GM-Brady, every success is "diagnostic" of his potential. When—after several failed attempts—he gets the syncopated harmony right, his accomplishment confirms that effective practice makes him better.

If a female student has a growth mindset, then STEM stereotypes don't much matter. She knows she can learn. If a Hispanic student has a GM, then ethnic stereotypes don't carry much weight. He knows he can improve.

In a sentence: a growth mindset makes stereotypes largely irrelevant.

"Brains Change" Research

These hypothetical descriptions sound plausible and make it easy to believe that mindset strategies solve ST problems. For psychologists to persuade us to adopt these practices, however, we'll need more than surface plausibility. In part I, we saw lots of persuasive research that a GM helps students learn generally. Here in part II, we need evidence that it specifically combats ST.

At the same time, because we've spent so much time exploring research paradigms, we probably don't need to see another ST study for each GM strategy on our list. A small sample can be helpfully persuasive. Two such studies can give us great confidence.

First: we know from chapter 3 that students adopt a GM when we teach them how brains change (Blackwell et al., 2007).

Following a similar logic, Catherine Good tested a multi-step hypothesis:

1. Learning that "brains change" promotes a growth mindset.
2. A GM lessens stereotype threat.
3. Therefore, a "brains change" lesson should help students shrug off stereotypes and learn more.

As you may remember from chapter 2, Good trained tutors to work with seventh graders. She had some of her tutors teach their students about the neural changes that take place during learning. They explained that "the mind is a muscle; the more you use it, the more it grows" (Good et al., 2003, p. 654).

To see what effect this growth-mindset approach had on ST, Good and her team examined year-end standardized test scores. On the state-wide math test, boys in a control group outscored girls by 7.5 points. However, when tutored to adopt a GM, girls' scores rose . . . by 8 points. In the end, the boys' scores in the GM tutoring group were not significantly higher than the girls' scores.

In other words: the initial gap between boys and girls did not result from the *students* but from the *climate* in which the students learned math. When the tutors created a new climate by promoting a GM, they stopped stereotype threat from taking hold. The girls did not feel their gender to be salient, and so they learned as much as the boys.

Good's team also explored academic stereotypes about ethnicity. In this school's cultural context, stereotypes held that Hispanic students couldn't learn English as well as their white peers. Yet here again, hearing that brains can change promoted a GM and thereby reduced ST. In Good's control group, Hispanic students averaged an 84.4 on the state-wide reading test. Those in the GM tutoring group averaged an 88.3. This notable improvement suggests that GM tutoring reduced the salience of ethnic stereotypes and—as with female math students—helped Hispanic students to read more fluently.

"Normalize Struggle" Research

The second study connecting GM with ST, honestly, is a blockbuster.

We've seen in chapter 2 that normalizing struggle promotes a GM. For that reason, it ought to reduce the effects of ST.

When Gregory Walton and Geoffrey Cohen tested that hypothesis, they found genuinely astonishing results (2011). Because their study included hundreds of students and lasted almost four years, we should pay careful attention to their methods and conclusions.

Walton and Cohen invited college freshmen to look at "survey data" that was—they were told—gathered from seniors at their current college. (In fact, the survey data had been made up.) According to this survey, these seniors had initially found the transition to college quite a challenge. They faced academic struggle, as well as social and emotional discombobulation.

These seniors' stories, like all good stories that normalize struggle, ended with success. Although they initially felt discomfort with a roommate, uncertainty about a group of friends, or dissatisfaction with romance, they ultimately felt academically confident and socially comfortable.

For example: one senior wrote, "Freshman year[,] even though I met large numbers of people, I didn't have a small group of close friends. . . . I was pretty homesick, and I had to remind myself that making close friends takes time. Since then . . . I have met people[,] some of whom are now just as close as my friends in high school were" (Walton & Cohen, 2011, p. 1448). Taken together, such comments emphasized that initial difficulties in college are typical and temporary. You can immediately recognize these techniques as part of the "normalize struggle" repertoire.

To ensure that the freshmen connected the survey data with their own college experience, Walton and Cohen asked them to write a brief essay. In this essay, they explained the struggles that they had already endured and envisioned a happier future: higher grades, hipper friends, happier roommates.

After this process, which lasted an hour or so, Walton and Cohen simply gathered data. *For four years.* Specifically, they tracked these students' GPAs and compared them to a control group: *all the other students in the college.*

Typically, a college student's GPA trends up over four years, so we should not be surprised to see such an increase. For the European American students in the control group (those students who did not go through Walton and Cohen's process), the average GPA increased 0.15 on a 4.0 scale: not a huge difference but laudable nonetheless. For the European American students in the study, the average GPA increased 0.20. This intervention didn't benefit these students all that much, but it certainly didn't hurt them.

Walton and Cohen's hypothesis focused on the African American students, and so they awaited these next numbers with heightened curiosity. For the African American students in the control group, the average GPA increased 0.07. For those in the study, their GPA rose more than 0.35. You read that right; their GPA rose *five times as much* as their control-group peers. Figure 6.1 tells a remarkable story.

Figure 6.1 compares those trend lines relative to each other. We can also look at the absolute numbers. Figure 6.2 shows that this one-hour intervention *cut the grade disparity in half* over four years.

Walton and Cohen tracked many other measures as well. Compared to the African Americans in the control group, those in the study were less likely to be in the bottom quarter of their class, more likely to be in the top quarter,

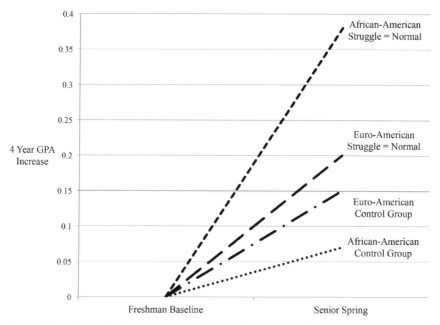

Figure 6.1. Change in College GPA with and without "Normalizing Struggle." *Adapted from "A Brief Social-Belonging Intervention Improves Academic and Health Outcomes of Minority Students," by G. M. Walton & G. L. Cohen, 2011, Science, 331(6023), p. 1448. Copyright 2011 by the American Association for the Advancement of Science.*

more likely to say they felt that they belonged at the school—even less likely to visit the doctor.

These dramatic results, at first, seem hard to believe. How can such a brief exercise—reading a made-up survey, writing a short essay—lead to such a striking change? Presumably, the exercise didn't have a single effect. Instead, it created a virtuous cycle.

Imagine, for example, that Kaylee battles with her freshman roommate. She borrows Kaylee's things and returns them damaged. She deliberately makes lots of noise when she gets up early to go jogging. Kaylee overhears her telling her friends that Kaylee is just a dullard.

Kaylee might start to suspect that her roommate just doesn't like gymnasts (or African Americans or Jews or Poles or transgender women or . . .). This suspicion makes her athleticism even more salient to her because she thinks every day about its effect on her rooming travails.

This increased salience has, in turn, at least two damaging effects. First, she starts to wonder if her other difficulties stem from her prowess on the uneven bars. Perhaps her history TA has never met a gymnast and just doesn't

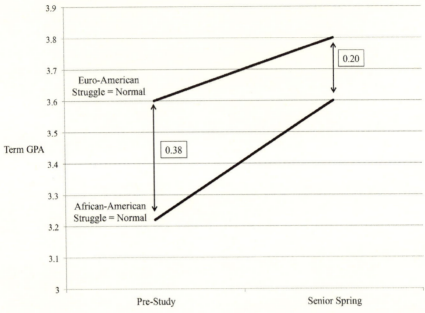

Figure 6.2. Change in GPA for European and African American Students after "Normalizing Struggle." Adapted from "A Brief Social-Belonging Intervention Improves Academic and Health Outcomes of Minority Students," by G. M. Walton & G. L. Cohen, 2011, Science, 331(6023), p. 1448. Copyright 2011 by the American Association for the Advancement of Science.

trust them. Perhaps she didn't make the a cappella group because of latent prejudice in the group.

Second, because of these repeated, stereotype-based difficulties, Kaylee begins to withdraw from the broader college community. She feels isolated and comfortable only with other gymnasts. They, at least, don't treat her badly for no reason.

In short: an early difficulty can make Kaylee's athletic passion especially salient to her, and that heightened salience leads to a vicious cycle of disappointment, greater salience, even greater disappointment, and so forth.

Walton and Cohen's strategy interrupts this cycle. When Kaylee first notices how badly her roommate treats her, she might start to attribute that animus to her athleticism. But when she recalls that such struggles are typical (after all, all those seniors had roommate difficulties) and temporary (no doubt, she'll get a new roommate next year), then she reroutes to a virtuous cycle instead.

Classroom Translations

To apply GM strategies in our own classrooms, we should begin with a review of part I, especially figure 3.4. As we tailor each strategy to our students and our own teaching personalities, we're automatically working against ST. So: strategy praise, a culture of error, and appropriate grading policies all foster the right kind of mindset and simultaneously reduce the salience of stereotypeable identity.

For example, Cody's Spanish teacher might offer this strategy praise: "I see you color-coded your flashcards when you studied this chapter's vocabulary. I bet that really helped you learn parts of speech very well."

The stereotype that "swimmers can't learn foreign languages" might still exist somewhere, but Cody's teacher has made it irrelevant. He clearly believes that Cody can learn and that this study strategy will help him do so. The limitations that might apply to swimmers have no space to breathe in this conversation.

The Walton and Cohen blockbuster study offers a highly translatable approach. These researchers gathered "data" from college seniors and shared it with freshmen. We can gather real data from our current students and share it with future students. At the end of a project or a unit, we can ask our third graders (or eighth graders or eleventh graders) about their challenges and their successes. We might structure this question as class feedback or as "letters to next year's class" or as an extra-credit assignment. No doubt they'll relate vivid stories about the difficulties that they faced and about their genuine pride at their accomplishments.

When we share these stories with future students, we should remember two key points in this method.

First, the struggle stories we share should end in success. The tale of the student who tried his best and never mastered the skill doesn't normalize struggle in a good way. We want students to see students who persevere and ultimately succeed.

Second, our students should not simply hear about prior challenges. Instead, they should spend time explicitly connecting those stories to their own experience. Walton and Cohen had their freshmen write an essay explaining how their experiences mirrored those of the seniors. You might lead small discussion groups or have students draw pictures or make comic books. Whatever method we choose, we should be sure that students make meaningful connections. They too have struggled. They too can predict success.

The Pink Elephant Problem

You've heard the problem before: if I ask you not to think about pink elephants, you automatically start thinking about them.

Psychologists have discovered one easy solution to this problem: *think about something else*. When tasked not to think about elephants, deliberately turn your thoughts to a topic that fascinates you: the Red Sox/Yankees rivalry, Silk Road history, Stephen Sondheim lyrics. Given freedom to obsess over a pet topic, your brain cheerfully putters off in its own direction and rarely returns to . . . what was the forbidden topic again?

When we want our students *not* to think about a particular part of their identities—the part that faces stereotypes—we face the pink-elephant problem. Perhaps, then, we can use the "think about something else" solution to help us and them out of this fix.

Researchers have tried this strategy, and it worked. Specifically, McGlone and Aronson encouraged students to focus on *prior academic successes* (2006). They suspected that by making classroom accomplishments salient, they could reduce the likelihood that gender (or race or religion or sexuality or . . .) would feel salient. Instead of thinking about the pink elephant of stereotype, our students would think about the Red Sox of their prior successes.

To study this possibility, McGlone tested a highly specific mental capacity: three-dimensional mental rotation. Imagine a figure built from eight or ten Lego pieces stuck together at different angles. It looks, perhaps, like a 3-D Tetris piece on steroids. Now, try to pivot that object in your mind. Look at it from several different angles. This "mental rotation" task turns out to be quite difficult to do. If you look online for practice problems, you'll be surprised by the challenge it poses.

McGlone tested 3-D mental rotation for a specific, even surprising, reason. Unlike almost all other cognitive capacities, 3-D mental rotation does show a substantial and consistent gender split (Hyde, 2005). In brief, men can rotate 3-D objects more accurately than women can. (MBE Principle #3 reminds us that averages apply to *groups, not individuals*. Men might be better than women on average, but *this* woman might be better than *that* man. For further discussion of this topic, including the source of this gender difference, see the FAQs at the end of chapter 7.)

McGlone asked several co-ed groups to take a 3-D mental rotation test. In the control group, as expected, men did better than women.

In his second group, McGlone wanted students to think about their gender. To make it salient, he instructed them to jot down three reasons someone might want to live in a co-ed college dormitory.

Sure enough, with heightened gender salience, men got better at 3-D mental rotation and women got worse. The stereotype that women don't have good spatial thinking skills wrought its Death Star devastation.

To make academic accomplishment salient, McGlone's third group of students wrote down three reasons that someone might want to attend an academically rigorous college. This group, presumably, spent less time thinking about gender and more time thinking about all the studying they had done to get where they were.

After pondering their school successes, both men and women improved at 3-D mental rotation. In fact, *women improved even more than the men did*. Because this intervention made positive parts of their identity salient, it crowded out the salience of gender-related stereotypes. Rather than think about pink elephants, they thought about all the work they had done to learn as much as they had.

Notice, by the way, that McGlone's writing prompts align with fixed and growth mindsets. When our students contemplate gender, they recognized a fixed part of themselves: one that (except in rare cases) will not change. When they contemplate academic success, they see how much they can develop over time. Most people are born either male or female, but no one is born a student at a demanding college.

This strategy, in other words, distracts students from thinking about *who they are* (fixed mindset) by inviting them to think about *what they have done* (growth mindset). Accentuating the positive automatically distracts from the negative.

Like other ST research paradigms we've studied, this one can be easily translated into our classrooms.

To focus his students on academic accomplishment, McGlone highlighted their admission to a competitive college. We might use a similar approach if our students have gotten into a selective AP course or an admission-only after-school program or a rigorous advanced section. "You worked hard simply to get into this class," we might say, "and experience tells me that continued hard work will help you learn this week's challenging topic." As our students recall their accomplishments, they have less brain real estate to focus on potential stereotypes.

Even without advanced programs or classes, we can almost certainly identify a relevant success to highlight for our students. "I know this spelling rule is a bear," I might say. "But I remember how well you mastered the last book we read. You have every reason to stay confident! We'll work on this together."

To make this approach work, we shouldn't simply do what McGlone did. After all, few of our students need to rotate 3-D objects or contemplate living in co-ed dorms. However, we can easily adapt his idea to our students' needs.

By adding and subtracting, by promoting a growth mindset, and by making students' accomplishments salient, we can disarm—even implode—the Death Star.

Figure 6.3 summarizes these anti-salience strategies.

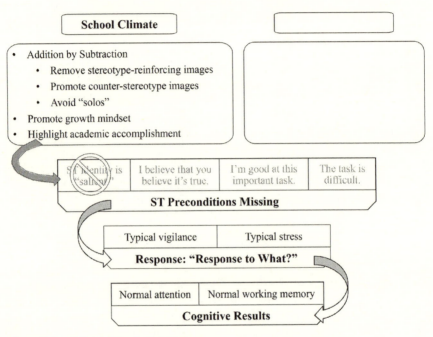

Figure 6.3. School Climate Solutions

Chapter Seven

Assessment and Stereotype Threat FAQs

Steele's theory, as we have seen, focuses less on individuals and more on social environments. In one climate, people function well: they can solve GRE problems and putt golf balls and rotate 3-D objects. In another, they bobble these tasks.

This broad focus naturally leads researchers to chapter 6's "climate change" strategies. When teachers promote ambient belonging, when we champion a growth mindset, when we hype prior successes, we create a school atmosphere that leaves little room for salience. Without salience, ST just never gets rolling.

ASSESSMENT STRATEGIES VS. STEREOTYPE THREAT

Our focus on salience also leads teachers to a second group of anti-ST strategies. Assessments, although intended to measure our students' progress and understanding, can themselves increase salience. Whenever a student faces a test—especially a high-stakes one—her thoughts reasonably turn to all the reasons she might struggle: the difficulty of the material, her best friend's habit of making distracting faces, even the nagging doubts raised by stereotypes.

Therefore, while we work on general "climate change" strategies, we should also think quite specifically about the ST dangers prompted by quizzes, tests, essays, presentations, and projects.

Psychology researchers have found ways for teachers to interrupt ST *before*, *during*, and *after* assessment.

Before

In part I, we repeatedly saw that small wording changes produced large learning differences. This guidance can shape our approach to tests as well.

In his very first study of ST, Steele told one student group that verbal GRE problems were "helpful practice." He told a second group that the problems "measured ability" (Steele & Aronson, 1995). After the second phrasing, as we saw in figure 5.2, the white students' average score doubled that of black students.

Presumably we can follow this guidance when we discuss upcoming tests with students. Rather than suggest we're testing innate ability ("We're about to find out who the real scientists are!"), we can instead frame a test as a beneficial chance to learn.

Adam Alter and colleagues have tested exactly this approach (Alter, Aronson, Darley, Rodriguez, & Ruble, 2010). They gave a math test to African American students who had been subtly reminded about academic stereotypes. Half of these students heard that the test would "show how good [they] were right now on this type of work," and thus "it would be able to measure [their] ability at solving math problems." This wording, of course, made stereotypes salient and emphasized a fixed mindset.

The second group heard that by taking this test they "would learn a lot of new things," and so "working on these problems might be a big help in school" (Alter et al., 2010, p. 167). By focusing on a growth mindset, these framing words worked against ST.

If we hadn't read Dweck's earlier research, we might be surprised to learn that these two-sentence introductions would matter very much. After all, math tests presumably measure a student's understanding of math and don't measure whatever the teacher said beforehand. Modest wording differences shouldn't change students' performance.

By now we're probably not so surprised. Alter's team tried this approach with both college students and middle schoolers. In both cases, the "helpful challenge" framework raised students' scores. When told that the test measured ability, for example, middle schoolers facing a stereotype scored 22 percent less than those for whom the stereotype wasn't salient. When told it would be "big help in school," that gap became statistically insignificant.

To make Alter's strategy work in our classrooms, we'll need to find just the right words that suit our voices and work with our students. You might say:

- "I learn best when I practice a new skill in many different ways. Tomorrow will give us all a different kind of practice!"
- "Friday's test has a fun new puzzle I really like. And I think you'll enjoy wrestling with it, too."

- "You remember how much we learned from the test on the last chapter. I bet that's going to happen with this one."

Of course, at times this strategy simply doesn't apply. Especially in older grades, students might well see a high-stakes test for what it is: not preparation for later understanding but a specific measurement that matters on its own. Students sitting for an Advanced Placement exam, presumably, focus less on the learning that will result from it and more on getting a five.

Your own teacherly instincts will guide you at these times. One class might like hearing an uplifting long-term perspective, in which case you can go right ahead and give it. Or they might sneer it away with adolescent hyperbole: "This test isn't helpful practice! It's the one exam that shapes the rest of my life!" In this case, you can use other stress-reducing techniques.

Alter's research provides a helpful suggestion, not an absolute commandment.

During

We can help reduce salience *before* a test with the words we use to describe it. We can reduce salience *during* a test with the structure of the test itself. Specifically, Annique Smeding has found that a test's starting point can make stereotypes salient.

Smeding asked French middle schoolers to take the Gallic version of the SAT. Half the students took the verbal section first, followed by the math; the other half reversed this order (Smeding, Dumas, Loose, & Régner, 2013). Her results reveal a quiet internal drama for the girls.

When a girl turned that first page and faced a *math* test, it seems, that page of numbers made the "girls-can't-do-math" stereotype salient. As a result, she strove to prove that presumption wrong. As we've seen time and again, the ineffective responses that flowed from her determination lowered her math test score.

Depressingly, her lack of math confidence then carried over to interfere with her subsequent *verbal* test—even though no stereotype suggests that girls do badly with words. For this reason, when they started with the math section, girls had low scores on both halves.

However, when a girl started with the *verbal* section, no such drama followed. The girls in this situation did just as well on verbal *and math* sections as the boys. (Test order made no difference for the boys, by the way.) With this research in mind, Smeding suggests that the SAT should always begin with the verbal section: an order that benefits girls without harming boys.

Sadly, teachers have little control over standardized tests. (If we did, we would start by placing demographic information at the test's *conclusion*. At that time, it would be too late to make stereotypeable identities salient.)

However, Smeding's research does suggest we contemplate the structure of our own tests. If possible, teachers might design assessments with several potential starting points—perhaps, sections I, II, and III. We could then instruct students to start the test *wherever they feel most confident*. The confidence that flows from this strong start, as seen in Smeding's study, prevents ST from taking hold and allows all students to demonstrate their understanding more effectively.

My English test, in other words, might have one section in which students identify quotations from *Macbeth*, a second in which they answer short questions, and a third essay section where they contrast King Duncan of Scotland and King Edward of England. A Latin test might have a vocabulary section, a section on second-declension nouns, and a short translation passage. Because such a test structure allows students to begin with their strength, they may well not worry about the stereotypes that would otherwise hover in the background.

For this strategy to work, of course, students need to know their choices in advance. We should not spring this structure on them as a surprise but let them know early on about the choices they'll have.

Equally important, we might recognize that a particular test or assignment doesn't allow for multiple entry places. If specific steps in a project must be done in order, then we can forgo this approach. As long as we're using some techniques to reduce salience, we don't need to force ourselves to try them all.

This multiple-starting-point approach highlights a broader point as well. When using this technique, teachers do not need to diagnose ST for individual students. We do not need to make one test for African American students, another for Evangelical students, another for female students, and then determine which student gets which test. By making one test with multiple entry points, we allow each student to build test confidence in whichever way works best.

The same point holds true for many techniques we've already discussed. When teachers normalize struggle, when we emphasize prior academic accomplishment, when we describe tests as beneficial challenges, we help all our students avoid ST without needing to presuppose which students feel which stereotype most keenly.

After

Before an assessment, we can (perhaps) frame it as a helpful challenge. *During* the assessment, we can (perhaps) let students start with their strengths.

After students take a test, however, teachers face an irksome paradox. If my students do badly on a test, I should—of course—give them specific feedback on what to do better. And yet, the more time I dwell on their mistakes, the more emphatically I evoke "secondhand belief." My focus on their errors gives students all the more reason to worry that I believe a stereotype.

At the same time, I can't *not* talk about their mistakes. If they did badly on a well-designed test, they most likely didn't learn the material. I shouldn't just pretend that everything is fine: "No, really, a 68 is a great score! No worries!"

In other words: I impede my students' learning if I don't review their mistakes, and I might make stereotypes salient if I do. How can I escape this dilemma?

Several scholars have located a clever escape hatch. A recent study led by David Yeager exemplifies this approach (Yeager et al., 2014).

Working with seventh-grade teachers, Yeager had students write a short essay about a personal hero. Teachers offered substantial and rigorous feedback on those essays and returned them to students.

The students received this feedback with a handwritten note attached. For half of the students, the note read, "I'm giving you these comments so that you'll have feedback on your paper." The other half got this note instead: "I'm giving you these comments because I have very high expectations and I know that you can reach them" (Yeager et al., 2014, p. 6). (The teachers did not know which students got which note.)

This second note includes two key components: an *explicit statement of high expectations* and a *certainty that the student can meet them*. Yeager and others call this combination "wise feedback," and its effectiveness belies its simplicity. In Yeager's study, African American students faced the stereotype that they are less academically accomplished than whites. The wise feedback they received, however, initiated a virtuous cycle—much like the cycle described in Walton and Cohen's study on normalizing struggle. In this case, wise feedback increased the African American students' confidence that their teachers believed in them and wanted them to succeed.

That is, it reduced stereotype salience.

As a result, whereas only 17 percent of the African American students who received the control feedback revised their essays, 71 percent of those who received wise feedback did so. Those revisions included twice as many corrections as did their peers' essays.

Unsurprisingly, extra revisions helped students learn. African American students who received the control feedback scored, on average, a 63 percent; those who received wise feedback averaged 79 percent—statistically indistinguishable from their white peers. Amazingly, wise feedback improved not only the grades on these assignments but also these students' year-end

GPA. Of course, the white students benefited from wise feedback. However, the African American students who faced disproportionate dangers from ST received concomitantly larger benefits from wise feedback.

Here again, as we've seen so often in motivation research, small changes have outsized benefits.

By the way, this strategy has been tested with many different frameworks for "high standards." Perhaps the *teacher* has the high standards. Perhaps the *department* or the *school* does. In one study, researchers invited students to compose an essay for a journal and alerted them that its editorial board had high standards (Cohen, Steele, & Ross, 1999).

This variety offers teachers good news. We can reasonably translate the wise feedback formula to fit our own classes. First graders might not much care that the district has high standards, but they very much care that you do.

As summarized in figure 7.1, teachers have many ways to create a general school climate that reduces ST and a specific assessment climate that does likewise.

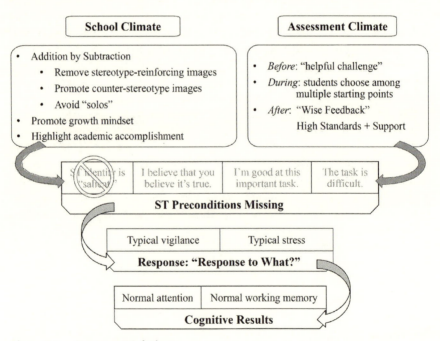

Figure 7.1. Assessment Solutions

BONUS STRATEGIES VS. ST

Although most ST solutions focus on reducing salience, researchers have explored other solutions as well. Two of them could work quite handily in our classrooms.

First, several researchers have explored the benefits of personal writing. In these studies, teachers typically give students a list of things they might value: friends, athletic success, family, religion, politics. Students rank these potential values according to their own priorities. They then write a personal essay about the one they value most: Why do they value friendship? What importance does politics have in their lives? How does athletics or religion connect them with others?

The specifics here might vary, but the goal remains the same: let students write about their own values, priorities, and lives. In fact, the technique is called "values affirmation." In some way or another, teachers let students explore their own value systems as part of their school experience.

We've got good evidence showing that this technique helps students generally and specifically helps students facing ST (Powers, Cook, Purdie-Vaughns, Garcia, Apfel, & Cohen, 2016; Shnabel, Purdie-Vaughns, Cook, Garcia, & Cohen, 2013). For instance, African American students who wrote about their own values ended the year with a higher GPA than others in a control group.

Here again, this strategy can be readily adapted to our own classrooms. Teachers in different grades, disciplines, and school systems can find different approaches to bring the idea to life. As long as the assignment lets each student express and explore her own values, it should help her feel more a part of the classroom and less subject to ST.

Most plausibly, this approach fits in our model at precondition #2. Students worry less that others believe stereotypes about them in classrooms that make room for their value systems. A sense of belonging buffers them from concerns about a potentially hostile environment.

A second bonus strategy draws on a very unusual research pool indeed.

As we've seen, stress is a key part of the ST system. It results from the preconditions and addles working memory and attention.

People respond to stress differently based on its perceived source. In one study, for example, researchers told students that they would be playing inaudible tones during an upcoming test (Ben-Zeev et al., 2005). That is, the notes were pitched so high that the participants probably wouldn't hear them. However, researchers told these students that even inaudible tones had been shown to increase stress when they take place. (Just to be clear: the researchers didn't really play tones—audible or otherwise.)

Students who took the subsequent test reported the same levels of stress as others who did not get this (very odd) cover story about inaudible tones. And yet, they did much better on the math test. Because they *attributed* their stress to an external source, one that didn't have meaning particular to them, it didn't interfere with their cognitive abilities as much.

Psychologist Michael Johns wondered if he could use this reattribution strategy to combat ST (Johns, Schmader, & Martens, 2005). Taking the stereotype bull by the horns, he reattributed women's math anxiety this way: "If you are feeling anxious while taking this test, this anxiety could be the result of those negative stereotypes that are widely known in society and have nothing to do with your actual ability to do well on this test" (Johns, Schmader, & Martens, 2005, p. 176). Without this guidance, women under ST scored dramatically lower than the men on a math test; with this guidance, the difference vanished.

This strategy seems counterintuitive—and not in a good way. By reminding students of stereotypes, we might well make those stereotypes salient. That is, this strategy deliberately highlights the very topic we've been trying to downplay.

For this reason, Johns's precise wording should get our attention. In the first place, he acknowledges that a stereotype exists, but he doesn't name it specifically. In the second place, he specifically notes that the stereotype, although "widely known in society," has "nothing to do with your actual ability." By reattributing the source of the stress, this technique reduces the damage that stress does to working memory and attention. The students can think of stereotypes as a barely audible background tone: one that needn't particularly worry them.

As always, you will know best whether this strategy makes sense for your students.

To many teachers, stereotype threat initially sounds like a terribly gloomy topic. It forces us to start difficult conversations and dwell on painful memories.

And yet, chapters 6 and 7 should have brightened the mood considerably. If we take time to understand the counterintuitive system by which ST operates, we can counteract—even defeat—its wiles.

In fact, we have a great many strategies to do so. Some strategies—those in the mindset category—offer benefits above and beyond ST reduction. And all of them leave plenty of room for teacherly flexibility and interpretation.

As we know from MBE principle #2, we should not strive to do precisely what these researchers did. Instead, we should understand their thought processes and then translate them to our unique teaching worlds. Every person reading this book will find different ways to put these strategies to use.

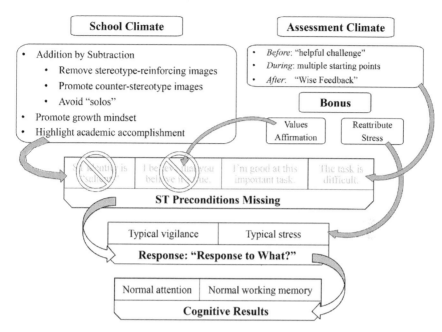

Figure 7.2. Bonus Solutions

They'll vary from grade to grade, country to country, teacher to teacher. And they work.

When we bring about the right kind of climate change, we see a direct and powerful result: greater motivation.

STEREOTYPE THREAT FAQS

1. Is there a "stereotype threat controversy" that resembles the "mindset controversy"?

Indeed.

We've already seen that, just as Kohn objects to mindset's focus on individual effort, many people object to ST's focus on community responsibility. I hope that, by this point, you agree with me that the two theories balance each other quite well. Students learn best as motivated (growth mindset) individuals within motivating (anti-stereotype threat) communities.

The replication crisis in psychology has also challenged ST research. Scholars have raised serious objections to ST methodology, and a lively debate is under way (for example, see Flore & Wicherts, 2015).

I myself am still on board, for the same reasons that I'm still persuaded by mindset research.

First, ST interventions clearly can help. In the Walton and Cohen study we explored (2011), African American students improved more than five times as much as peers in a control group. This study measured hundreds of people over four years. Those are robust numbers indeed.

Second, ST theory doesn't need to eliminate group differences completely to be helpful. If ST strategies make small differences over time, they can add up to large meaningful effects (Walton & Spencer, 2009).

Third, neuroscience research does bolster the psychology studies we've seen. If ST doesn't happen, it's surprising that the brains Krendl studied behaved as they did (Krendl et al., 2008).

To be clear: science works well because it updates itself based on good evidence. If the evidence in ST's favor doesn't substantially outweigh the evidence against it, then we all—including me—should not give it further credence. At present, my reading of current research gives me confidence to write these chapters. If I ever change my mind, I'll be quite public about doing so.

2. Most of the stereotypes discussed here fall into two categories: (1) women in STEM disciplines and (2) U.S. racial and ethnic minorities facing academic challenges. Can you offer another example? Maybe even one outside of the United States?

I recently discussed ST with teachers at an international school far away from the American continents. Some teachers there had contemplated starting an honor code but wondered if it might create ST problems. We used figure 7.2 to structure our discussion of this intriguing question.

First, because an honor code makes the topic of *cheating* salient, we should ask: Are there relevant stereotypes? In this particular social context, are some identifiable groups stereotyped to be less honest than others?

This question has particular weight in an international school, which by design brings together students from many different cultural backgrounds. We had to consider American stereotypes (the school largely serves American students abroad) *and* the local country's stereotypes *and* stereotypes held by different cultures represented at the school.

After some discussion, we concluded that, *yes*, in this school's population, one clearly identifiable group did face a stereotype about honesty.

Given that background, we then explored ST preconditions.

- Would signing an honor-code pledge make this stereotype more *salient*? We know that simply checking demographic boxes before standardized tests can do so. It seems quite plausible that signing a pledge would do so as well.

- Might students *believe that others believe*? Again, that concern sounds plausible. If stereotypes hold that my people are naturally dishonest, and you ask me to sign a pledge of honesty, your request might make me think you doubt me. (We should remember the question is not "Do the teachers at this school think that this group of students is dishonest?" but "Could the students in the group reasonably believe that teachers believe the stereotype?" Even if the teachers have never heard of this stereotype, ST will still interfere with learning if students fear they believe it.)
- Do these students *care about doing well*? Surely many of them do, much of the time.
- Is the work *difficult*? Surely some of it is, some of the time.

If the four preconditions are met, how could they lead to ineffective responses?

- In our discussion, we could easily imagine these students becoming increasingly *internally vigilant*. Because they want to prove the stereotype wrong, they might constantly worry about the honesty of their actions. "The instructions say that I may look at my notes. But I got some of these notes from my friend. Is it cheating to look at those too?" "I'm allowed to use a calculator, but my calculator has advanced programming functions. That just might be unfair . . ."
- We could also imagine them being *externally vigilant*. Students who sign an honor code might be allowed to take tests on their own. Would they worry if they see a teacher walk by? ("She's monitoring me more than others; she doesn't trust me.")
- In both cases, all this vigilance could quite easily raise *stress* levels.

In turn, these ineffective responses might well upend cognitive functions. With their *attention distracted* by all those needless worries and *working memory overwhelmed* by these extra concerns, we can easily imagine these students falling short of their academic potential.

Clearly, then, cultural stereotypes about honesty should influence a school's decision about starting an honor code.

However, those concerns don't necessarily preclude an honor code. Instead, they encourage us to review chapters 6 and 7 for relevant solutions. Can we ensure our classrooms include images of famously honest people? Can we create a growth mindset around honesty? Can we highlight students' other accomplishments, so they're not thinking about this stereotype?

ST research doesn't tell schools and teachers precisely what to do. Instead, it offers us new ways to think through old problems. If this school chooses to implement an honor code, that code will be better because of the time teachers took to rethink these questions from a ST perspective.

(By the way: if you're interested in honor codes, Dan Ariely's book about dishonesty does a great job making complex research accessible and useful [2012].)

3. Do stereotypes ever benefit people? If yes, should we use them to do so?
Yes, and no.

When we remind men or Asian students about math stereotypes in their favor, they do score marginally higher on math tests (Mendoza-Denton, Kahn, & Chan, 2008).

However, I don't think we should use this effect—called "stereotype lift"—as a teaching strategy. We want our students to do well on math tests not because they're temporarily given a shot of stereotyped confidence but because they understand the math. (For more on stereotype lift, see Walton & Cohen, 2003.)

4. If a student has a diagnosed LD, won't most assessments make stereotypes even more salient*? If that's true, then tests automatically start the ST machinery for these students.*

Oddly, I've never found any research that specifically addresses ST and learning differences. For this reason, I know of no research-based way out of this conundrum.

My optimistic suggestion is this: explore non-assessment assessments to track your student's progress. Here's what I mean:

Students can demonstrate their understanding many different ways. If your student helps a classmate solve a problem or gets a tricky homework problem correct or explains a concept to you lucidly, you might well conclude that he understands this topic well.

If he subsequently belly-flops on a test, you might change your mind. Or you might conclude that the test wasn't the right way to measure his (otherwise obvious) understanding. The problem isn't in the individual; he understands. The problem is in the school environment; the test doesn't accurately measure his understanding.

Given this specific student's learning profile, you might let other measures guide your evaluation. His success on low-stakes homework or in informal peer-tutoring sessions might shape the grade he gets in your class.

To be clear: I'm not suggesting that we abandon our standards and simply give everyone an A just for trying. I am suggesting that tests might accurately measure some students *but not others*. We needn't focus exclusively on the question: "How well did this student do on this test?" We can also ask: "How well does she understand the material? Does she have the right opportunities to show what she does understand?"

As always, MBE principle #1 plays an important role here. I know of no ST researcher who says, "You must *do this* with your LD students." Instead, ST research invites you to think in a new way about your work with them. If you worry that assessments make their learning differences salient, then you might look for a work-around. You might measure their understanding in some way that *both* upholds relevant standards *and* protects them from ST. Only you, as the classroom teacher, know how best to accomplish that joint mission.

5. This isn't PC of me to ask, but what if a stereotype is true? What if X group really is better at learning something than Y group? You yourself said that men are better than women at 3-D mental rotation.

As a teacher, my job is to help this student right here learn more. Every second I focus on a stereotype's potential validity is a second I'm not doing so.

In other words: we might debate whether difficulty with 3-D mental rotation impedes (say) geometry learning. We might debate the source of gender differences in that ability.

This point seems beyond debate: all these other debates ultimately distract me from my job. I should work as hard as I can to help this student learn this material.

6. I teach fourth grade, with a focus on social studies. Who can tell me exactly what these ST strategies should look like in my classroom?

You can.

Let me be more emphatic about that. If other people say with great certainty that they can answer your question, their confidence should make you skeptical.

Here's an example. In a recent ST presentation, I stressed the importance of normalizing struggle: "If you know that an upcoming topic will pose real difficulties, you might let your students know. When they perceive struggle to be normal, they don't attribute their own difficulties to the stereotype."

In the small-group discussions that followed, I overheard a teacher say this: "I would *never* tell my students to expect a topic to be difficult. That sounds so *gloomy*. Instead, I would say 'I know how much you like a challenge, and so I'm sure you'll really enjoy this next chapter.' That's a much better way to make the same point."

This teacher, quite splendidly, found a way to translate generic advice ("normalize struggle") into her own voice. By reminding her students "how much they like a challenge," she both prepares them for the rigors of the upcoming chapter and does so with the optimism that fits her persona.

However, that same phrasing might not work for you at all. You might be the "tough love" teacher. You might have a class that really does not like a challenge and wouldn't be fooled by your pretense that they do. You might have a colleague who uses that exact phrasing and therefore want to avoid reduplication.

Hence MBE principle #2: don't obey; don't imitate. Instead, review figure 7.2 and translate that research into words and teaching strategies that work for you.

If you trust other fourth-grade teachers or experienced colleagues or wise mentors, you might solicit their ideas. We almost always benefit from the experience of others. Their thoughts, like those summarized in this book, should guide you but not limit you.

7. You've told me to avoid "solos." But I've got only one student of color in my class; she's from Indonesia. What can I do?

In the first place, her solo status matters only if she faces a relevant stereotype. If not, you have no need to worry.

If such a stereotype exists, then use the strategies you've got as best you can. If she must be solo, you might seek out pictures of famously successful Indonesians. (Susi Pudjiastuti ran a successful business before she became a minister in the Indonesian government—even though she never graduated from high school.) You can normalize struggle. You can offer wise feedback. You've got many ways to reduce salience; use the ones that will be most effective for your students.

8. I have a question about a specific study. Shouldn't we just teach our students about Steele's theory? Wouldn't they benefit from knowing about ST? Isn't that what Johns's study really shows?

Johns used very specific language with his students: "If you are feeling anxious while taking this test, this anxiety could be the result of those negative stereotypes that are widely known in society and have nothing to do with your actual ability to do well on this test." He quite carefully did not mention the actual stereotype: "Men are better than women at math."

For this reason, we don't have a research-based answer. True, some schools work to defeat ST by directly confronting stereotypes. If you favor this approach, many scholars have summarized anti-stereotype research in helpful ways (Eliot, 2009; Hyde, 2005).

You might just as easily infer from Johns's paradigm that downplaying the specifics of the stereotype benefits students. After all, he kept his phrasing quite vague: "those negative stereotypes that are widely known in society."

If this second approach sounds right in your classroom, you might deliberately keep your warning at a distance. Early in the year, you might say something like this: "You know, we live in a society that has lots of stereotypes about who is good or bad at what. Sometimes they make us anxious. I want you to know that none of those beliefs matters here. In this room, we will all make lots of mistakes and also lots of progress."

You will find your own time and your own words to make this brief speech. In any case, it can be part of your anti-ST repertoire, not the only strategy you've got.

In chapter 3, I argued that knowing mindset lingo probably won't help students because it's too abstract. Rather than take class time to talk about a growth mindset, I'd rather just use the strategies that promote it. I have similar thoughts about ST. In the absence of specific research, I'm just skeptical that students will know how to use ST terminology to help themselves learn. Even teachers often find these counterintuitive ideas hard to process.

As always, the classroom teacher gets the final word. You know your students and yourself; you now know ST research better than most people on the planet. If you believe that teaching Steele's theory will benefit your students, by all means do so. (If you do, try to get a researcher involved. Your classroom might make a fascinating study!)

9. The first book in the series was about working memory *and* attention. *This one is about* motivation. *What's next?*

Learning Thrives explores fascinating research into long-term memory formation. We'll look at the neuro-biological basis of memory and strategies that help students encode and retrieve new memories. It's an enthralling and rapidly evolving field and brings together the concepts and suggestions explored in the first two books.

I look forward to seeing you there.

References

Alter, A. L., Aronson, J., Darley, J. M., Rodriguez, C., & Ruble, D. N. (2010). Rising to the threat: Reducing stereotype threat by reframing the threat as a challenge. *Journal of Experimental Social Psychology, 46*(1), 166–171.

Amemiya, J., & Wang, M. T. (2018). Why effort praise can backfire in adolescence. *Child Development Perspectives, 12*(3), 199–203. doi.org/10.1111/cdep.12284.

Ames, C., & Archer, J. (1988). Achievement goals in the classroom: Students' learning strategies and motivation processes. *Journal of Educational Psychology, 80*(3), 260–267.

Appel, M., & Kronberger, N. (2012). Stereotypes and the achievement gap: Stereotype threat prior to test taking. *Educational Psychology Review, 24*(4), 609–635.

Ariely, D. (2012). *The (honest) truth about dishonesty: How we lie to everyone—especially ourselves*. New York: Harper Perennial.

Aronson, J., Fried, C. B., & Good, C. (2002). Reducing the effects of stereotype threat on African American college students by shaping theories of intelligence. *Journal of Experimental Social Psychology, 38*(2), 113–125.

Aronson, J., Lustina, M. J., Good, C., Keough, K., Steele, C. M., & Brown, J. (1999). When white men can't do math: Necessary and sufficient factors in stereotype threat. *Journal of Experimental Social Psychology, 35*(1), 29–46.

Barber, S. J., & Mather, M. (2013). Stereotype threat can both enhance and impair older adults' memory. *Psychological Science, 24*(12), 2522–2529.

Baumeister, R. F., & Tierney, J. (2011). *Willpower: Rediscovering the greatest human strength*. New York: Penguin.

Beilock, S. L., Jellison, W. A., Rydell, R. J., McConnell, A. R., & Carr, T. H. (2006). On the causal mechanisms of stereotype threat: Can skills that don't rely heavily on working memory still be threatened? *Personality and Social Psychology Bulletin, 32*(8), 1059–1071.

Beilock, S. L., Rydell, R. J., & McConnell, A. R. (2007). Stereotype threat and working memory: Mechanisms, alleviation, and spillover. *Journal of Experimental Psychology: General, 136*(2), 256–276.

Ben-Zeev, T., Fein, S., & Inzlicht, M. (2005). Arousal and stereotype threat. *Journal of Experimental Social Psychology, 41*(2), 174–181.

Bjork, E. L., & Bjork, R. A. (2014). Making things hard on yourself, but in a good way: Creating desirable difficulties to enhance learning. In M. A. Gernsbacher and J. Pomerantz (Eds.), *Psychology and the real world: Essays illustrating fundamental contributions to society*, 2nd edition (pp. 59–68). New York: Worth.

Blackwell, L. S., Trzesniewski, K. H., & Dweck, C. S. (2007). Implicit theories of intelligence predict achievement across an adolescent transition: A longitudinal study and an intervention. *Child Development, 78*(1), 246–263.

Blascovich, J., Spencer, S. J., Quinn, D., & Steele, C. (2001). African Americans and high blood pressure: The role of stereotype threat. *Psychological Science, 12*(3), 225–229.

Boaler, J. (2016). *Mathematical mindsets: Unleashing students' potential through creative math, inspiring messages, and innovative teaching.* San Francisco: Jossey-Bass.

Bosson, J. K., Haymovitz, E. L., & Pinel, E. C. (2004). When saying and doing diverge: The effects of stereotype threat on self-reported versus non-verbal anxiety. *Journal of Experimental Social Psychology, 40*(2), 247–255.

Brown, P. C., Roediger, H. L. III, & McDaniel, M. A. (2014). *Make it stick: The science of successful learning.* Cambridge, Mass.: The Belknap Press of Harvard University Press.

Brummelman, E., Thomaes, S., Overbeek, G., Orobio de Castro, B., Van Den Hout, M. A., & Bushman, B. J. (2014). On feeding those hungry for praise: Person praise backfires in children with low self-esteem. *Journal of Experimental Psychology: General, 143*(1), 9–14.

Burnette, J. L., O'Boyle, E. H., VanEpps, E. M., Pollack, J. M., & Finkel, E. J. (2013). Mind-sets matter: A meta-analytic review of implicit theories and self-regulation. *Psychological Bulletin, 139*(3), 655–701.

Camerer, C. F., Dreber, A., Holzmeister, F., Ho, T. H., Huber, J., Johannesson, M., . . . & Wu, H. (2018). Evaluating the replicability of social science experiments in *Nature* and *Science* between 2010 and 2015. *Nature Human Behaviour, 2*, 637–644.

Cherney, I. D. (2008). Mom, let me play more computer games: They improve my mental rotation skills. *Sex Roles, 59*(11–12), 776–786.

Cheryan, S., Plaut, V. C., Davies, P. G., & Steele, C. M. (2009). Ambient belonging: How stereotypical cues impact gender participation in computer science. *Journal of Personality and Social Psychology, 97*(6), 1045–1060.

Cimpian, A., Arce, H. M. C., Markman, E. M., & Dweck, C. S. (2007). Subtle linguistic cues affect children's motivation. *Psychological Science, 18*(4), 314–316.

Claro, S., & Loeb, S. (2017). *New evidence that students' beliefs about their brains drive learning* (Evidence Speaks Reports, Vol 2, #29). Retrieved from Brookings Institution website: www.brookings.edu/wp-content/uploads/2017/11/claro-and-loeb-report.pdf.

Cohen, G. L., Garcia, J., Apfel, N., & Master, A. (2006). Reducing the racial achievement gap: A social-psychological intervention. *Science, 313*(5791), 1307–1310.

Cohen, G. L., Steele, C. M., & Ross, L. D. (1999). The mentor's dilemma: Providing critical feedback across the racial divide. *Personality and Social Psychology Bulletin, 25*(10), 1302–1318.

Crandall, V. C., Katkovsky, W., & Crandall, V. J. (1965). Children's beliefs in their own control of reinforcements in intellectual-academic achievement situations. *Child Development, 36*(1), 91–109.

Croizet, J. C., Després, G., Gauzins, M. E., Huguet, P., Leyens, J. P., & Méot, A. (2004). Stereotype threat undermines intellectual performance by triggering a disruptive mental load. *Personality and Social Psychology Bulletin, 30*(6), 721–731.

Dasgupta, N., Scircle, M. M., & Hunsinger, M. (2015). Female peers in small work groups enhance women's motivation, verbal participation, and career aspirations in engineering. *Proceedings of the National Academy of Sciences, 112*(16), 4988–4993.

Dear Parents. (2017). Retrieved July 14, 2018, from i.imgur.com/HFzlJSF.jpg.

Diener, C. I., & Dweck, C. S. (1978). An analysis of learned helplessness: Continuous changes in performance, strategy, and achievement cognitions following failure. *Journal of Personality and Social Psychology, 36*(5), 451–462.

———. (1980). An analysis of learned helplessness: II. The processing of success. *Journal of Personality and Social Psychology, 39*(5), 940–952.

Dweck, C. S. (2000). *Self-theories: Their role in motivation, personality, and development.* New York: Psychology Press.

———. (2006). *Mindset: The new psychology of success: How we can learn to fulfill our potential.* New York: Ballantine.

Dweck, C. S., Chiu, C. Y., & Hong, Y. Y. (1995). Implicit theories and their role in judgments and reactions: A word from two perspectives. *Psychological Inquiry, 6*(4), 267–285.

Dweck, C. S., & Leggett, E. L. (1988). A social-cognitive approach to motivation and personality. *Psychological Review, 95*(2), 256–273.

Dweck, C. S., & Sorich, L. A. (1999). Mastery-oriented thinking. In C. R. Snyder (Ed.), *Coping: The psychology of what works* (pp. 232–251). New York: Oxford University Press.

Editorial: Motivational processes affecting learning. (1986). *American Psychologist, 41*(10), 1040.

Eliot, L. (2009). *Pink brain, blue brain: How small differences grow into troublesome gaps—and what we can do about it.* Boston: Houghton Mifflin Harcourt.

Elliot, A. J. (1999). Approach and avoidance motivation and achievement goals. *Educational Psychologist, 34*(3), 169–189.

Elliott, E. S., & Dweck, C. S. (1988). Goals: An approach to motivation and achievement. *Journal of Personality and Social Psychology, 54*(1), 5–12.

Erdley, C. A., Loomis, C. C., Cain, K. M., Dumas-Hines, F., & Dweck, C. (1997). Relations among children's social goals, implicit personality theories, and responses to social failure. *Developmental Psychology, 33*(2), 263–272.

Flore, P. C., & Wicherts, J. M. (2015). Does stereotype threat influence performance of girls in stereotyped domains? A meta-analysis. *Journal of School Psychology, 53*(1), 25–44.

Good, C., Aronson, J., & Inzlicht, M. (2003). Improving adolescents' standardized test performance: An intervention to reduce the effects of stereotype threat. *Journal of Applied Developmental Psychology, 24*(6), 645–662.

Grant, H., & Dweck, C. S. (2003). Clarifying achievement goals and their impact. *Journal of Personality and Social Psychology, 85*(3), 541–553.

Heine, S. J., Kitayama, S., Lehman, D. R., Takata, T., Ide, E., Leung, C., & Matsumoto, H. (2001). Divergent consequences of success and failure in Japan and North America: An investigation of self-improving motivations and malleable selves. *Journal of Personality and Social Psychology, 81*(4), 599–615.

Henderson, V. L., & Dweck, C. S. (1990). Motivation and achievement. In S. S. Feldman & G. R. Elliott (Eds.), *At the threshold: The developing adolescent* (pp. 308–329). Cambridge, Mass.: Harvard University Press.

Henrich, J., Heine, S., & Norenzayan, A. (2010). The weirdest people in the world? *Behavioral and Brain Sciences, 33*(2–3), 61–83.

Heyman, G. D., Dweck, C. S., & Cain, K. M. (1992). Young children's vulnerability to self–blame and helplessness: Relationship to beliefs about goodness. *Child Development, 63*(2), 401–415.

Hong, Y. Y., Chiu, C. Y., Dweck, C. S., Lin, D. M. S., & Wan, W. (1999). Implicit theories, attributions, and coping: A meaning system approach. *Journal of Personality and Social Psychology, 77*(3), 588–599.

Hutchison, K. A., Smith, J. L., & Ferris, A. (2013). Goals can be threatened to extinction: Using the Stroop task to clarify working memory depletion under stereotype threat. *Social Psychological and Personality Science, 4*(1), 74–81.

Hyde, J. S. (2005). The gender similarities hypothesis. *American Psychologist, 60*(6), 581–592.

Johns, M., Inzlicht, M., & Schmader, T. (2008). Stereotype threat and executive resource depletion: Examining the influence of emotion regulation. *Journal of Experimental Psychology: General, 137*(4), 691.

Johns, M., Schmader, T., & Martens, A. (2005). Knowing is half the battle: Teaching stereotype threat as a means of improving women's math performance. *Psychological Science, 16*(3), 175–179.

Kohn, A. (2015). The perils of "Growth Mindset" education: Why we're trying to fix our kids when we should be fixing the system: How a promising but oversimplified idea caught fire, then got co-opted by conservative ideology. *Salon*. Retrieved from www.salon.com/2015/08/16/the_education_fad_thats_hurting_our_kids_what_you_need_to_know_about_growth_mindset_theory_and_the_harmful_lessons_it_imparts/

Krendl, A. C., Richeson, J. A., Kelley, W. M., & Heatherton, T. F. (2008). The negative consequences of threat: A functional magnetic resonance imaging investigation of the neural mechanisms underlying women's underperformance in math. *Psychological Science, 19*(2), 168–175.

Lemov, D. (2015). *Teach like a champion, 2.0: 62 techniques that put students on the path to college*. San Francisco: Jossey-Bass.

Leyens, J. P., Désert, M., Croizet, J. C., & Darcis, C. (2000). Stereotype threat: Are lower status and history of stigmatization preconditions of stereotype threat? *Personality and Social Psychology Bulletin, 26*(10), 1189–1199.

Lin-Siegler, X., Ahn, J. N., Chen, J., Fang, F. F. A., & Luna-Lucero, M. (2016). Even Einstein struggled: Effects of learning about great scientists' struggles on high school students' motivation to learn science. *Journal of Educational Psychology, 108*(3), 314–328.

Mangels, J. A., Butterfield, B., Lamb, J., Good, C., & Dweck, C. S. (2006). Why do beliefs about intelligence influence learning success? A social cognitive neuroscience model. *Social Cognitive and Affective Neuroscience, 1*(2), 75–86.

Martocchio, J. J. (1994). Effects of conceptions of ability on anxiety, self-efficacy, and learning in training. *Journal of Applied Psychology, 79*(6), 819–825.

Master, A., Cheryan, S., & Meltzoff, A. N. (2016). Computing whether she belongs: Stereotypes undermine girls' interest and sense of belonging in computer science. *Journal of Educational Psychology, 108*(3), 424–437.

McGlone, M. S., & Aronson, J. (2006). Stereotype threat, identity salience, and spatial reasoning. *Journal of Applied Developmental Psychology, 27*(5), 486–493.

McIntyre, R. B., Paulson, R. M., & Lord, C. G. (2003). Alleviating women's mathematics stereotype threat through salience of group achievements. *Journal of Experimental Social Psychology, 39*(1), 83–90.

Mendoza-Denton, R., Kahn, K., & Chan, W. (2008). Can fixed views of ability boost performance in the context of favorable stereotypes? *Journal of Experimental Social Psychology, 44*(4), 1187–1193.

Mueller, C. M., & Dweck, C. S. (1998). Praise for intelligence can undermine children's motivation and performance. *Journal of Personality and Social Psychology, 75*(1), 33–52.

Murphy, M. C., Steele, C. M., & Gross, J. J. (2007). Signaling threat: How situational cues affect women in math, science, and engineering settings. *Psychological Science, 18*(10), 879–885.

NickSoderstrom. (2018, March 5). My concern that growth mindset is becoming the new learning styles is growing. Tweet. Retrieved from twitter.com/NickSoderstrom/status/970817896757776392.

Nisbett, R. E. (2003). *The geography of thought: How Asians and Westerners think differently . . . and why*. New York: Free Press.

———. (2009). *Intelligence and how to get it: Why schools and cultures count*. New York: W. W. Norton & Company.

O'Rourke, E., Haimovitz, K., Ballweber, C., Dweck, C., & Popović, Z. (2014, April). Brain points: A growth mindset incentive structure boosts persistence in an educational game. In *Proceedings of the SIGCHI conference on human factors in computing systems* (pp. 3339–3348). ACM.

Park, D., Gunderson, E. A., Tsukayama, E., Levine, S. C., & Beilock, S. L. (2016). Young children's motivational frameworks and math achievement: Relation to teacher-reported instructional practices, but not teacher theory of intelligence. *Journal of Educational Psychology, 108*(3), 300–313.

Pashler, H., McDaniel, M., Rohrer, D., & Bjork, R. (2008). Learning styles: Concepts and evidence. *Psychological Science in the Public Interest, 9*(3), 105–119.

Porter, T., & Schumann, K. (2018). Intellectual humility and openness to the opposing view. *Self and Identity, 17*(2), 139–162.

Powers, J. T., Cook, J. E., Purdie-Vaughns, V., Garcia, J., Apfel, N., & Cohen, G. L. (2016). Changing environments by changing individuals: The emergent effects of psychological intervention. *Psychological Science, 27*(2), 150–160.

Rattan, A., Good, C., & Dweck, C. S. (2012). "It's ok—not everyone can be good at math": Instructors with an entity theory comfort (and demotivate) students. *Journal of Experimental Social Psychology, 48*(3), 731–737.

Robins, R. W., & Pals, J. L. (2002). Implicit self-theories in the academic domain: Implications for goal orientation, attributions, affect, and self-esteem change. *Self and Identity, 1*(4), 313–336.

Rose, T. (2016). *The end of average: How we succeed in a world that values sameness.* New York: HarperCollins Publishers.

Sarrasin, J. B., Nenciovici, L., Foisy, L. M. B., Allaire-Duquette, G., Riopel, M., & Masson, S. (2018). Effects of teaching the concept of neuroplasticity to induce a growth mindset on motivation, achievement, and brain activity: A meta-analysis. *Trends in Neuroscience and Education, 12,* 22–31.

Sarrazin, P., Biddle, S., Famose, J. P., Cury, F., Fox, K., & Durand, M. (1996). Goal orientations and conceptions of the nature of sport ability in children: A social cognitive approach. *British Journal of Social Psychology, 35*(3), 399–414.

Schmader, T., Johns, M., & Forbes, C. (2008). An integrated process model of stereotype threat effects on performance. *Psychological Review, 115*(2), 336–356.

Sekaquaptewa, D., & Thompson, M. (2003). Solo status, stereotype threat, and performance expectancies: Their effects on women's performance. *Journal of Experimental Social Psychology, 39*(1), 68–74.

Shih, M., Pittinsky, T. L., & Ambady, N. (1999). Stereotype susceptibility: Identity salience and shifts in quantitative performance. *Psychological Science, 10*(1), 80–83.

Shnabel, N., Purdie-Vaughns, V., Cook, J. E., Garcia, J., & Cohen, G. L. (2013). Demystifying values-affirmation interventions: Writing about social belonging is a key to buffering against identity threat. *Personality and Social Psychology Bulletin, 39*(5), 663–676.

Sisk, V. F., Burgoyne, A. P., Sun, J., Butler, J. L., & Macnamara, B. N. (2018). To what extent and under which circumstances are growth mind-sets important to academic achievement? Two meta-analyses. *Psychological Science, 29*(4), 549–571.

Smeding, A., Dumas, F., Loose, F., & Régner, I. (2013). Order of administration of math and verbal tests: An ecological intervention to reduce stereotype threat on girls' math performance. *Journal of Educational Psychology, 105*(3), 850–860.

Smiley, P. A., & Dweck, C. S. (1994). Individual differences in achievement goals among young children. *Child Development, 65*(6), 1723–1743.

Steele, C. (2010). *Whistling Vivaldi: How stereotypes affect us and what we can do.* New York: W. W. Norton & Co.

Steele, C. M., & Aronson, J. (1995). Stereotype threat and the intellectual test performance of African Americans. *Journal of Personality and Social Psychology, 69*(5), 797–811.

Stevenson, H. W., Chen, C., & Lee, S. Y. (1993). Mathematics achievement of Chinese, Japanese, and American children: Ten years later. *Science, 231,* 693–699.

Stipek, D., & Gralinski, J. H. (1996). Children's beliefs about intelligence and school performance. *Journal of Educational Psychology, 88*(3), 397–407.

Walton, G. M., & Cohen, G. L. (2003). Stereotype lift. *Journal of Experimental Social Psychology, 39*(5), 456–467.

———. (2011). A brief social-belonging intervention improves academic and health outcomes of minority students. *Science, 331*(6023), 1447–1451.

Walton, G. M., & Spencer, S. J. (2009). Latent ability: Grades and test scores systematically underestimate the intellectual ability of negatively stereotyped students. *Psychological Science, 20*(9), 1132–1139.

Watson, A. (2017). *Learning begins: The science of working memory and attention for the classroom teacher*. Lanham, Md.: Rowman & Littlefield.

Willingham, D. (2009). *Why don't students like school? A cognitive scientist answers questions about how the mind works and what it means for the classroom*. San Francisco: Jossey-Bass.

Yeager, D. S., Purdie-Vaughns, V., Garcia, J., Apfel, N., Brzustoski, P., Master, A., . . . & Cohen, G. L. (2014). Breaking the cycle of mistrust: Wise interventions to provide critical feedback across the racial divide. *Journal of Experimental Psychology: General, 143*(2), 804–824.

Index

Page references for figures are italicized.

3-D mental rotation, 124, 139

ability/effort. *See* step 3
African Leadership Academy, 78–79
ambient belonging, 113–14
assessment. *See* grades and grading
assessment strategies: after, 130–32, *132*; before, 127–29, *132*; during, 129–30, *132*
attention, xii, xvi, xix, 58, 141; and stereotype threat, 98, 101–2, *104*, 107, 111–12, 133–34, 137

Badman method, 24, 26–27
Boaler, Jo, 44, 65–66
body language, 100

charge/retreat. *See* step 4

Daniel, 6–7, 67–69
desirable difficulties, 3–4
"diagnostic," 78–79, 118
disciplinary mindset, 66–67, *69*
dishonesty, 20

goals, performance and learning. *See* step 2
grades and grading, 52–54, *53*, *57*, 58–59, 61–64, 68, *69*, 81, 138
grit, 78, 111

kindness, dangers of, 24, 26–27, *29*
Kohn, Alfie, 71–73, 108, 135

learning differences, 138–39

meta-analysis, 73–75
microsweating, 100
mind, brain, and education, xv, xvi, xx; principle #1, xvii, 39, 139; principle #2, xvii, 21, 27, 44, 59, 115, 123, 125, 128–29, 133–35, 139–40; principle #3, xviii, 124
mindset, fixed and growth. *See* step 1
mindset terminology, 80
Monty Python's The Holy Grail, 5

neuroscience, 44–45, 54–57, 73, 81, 90–91, 136

normalizing struggle, 36–44, *45*, 119–20, *121–22*, 123, 130, 139
"no solos," 116, *126*, 140

praise, person vs. process, 16–25, 29, *29*, 68, 72, 123; grammatical form of, 23; "precise," 21–22

reattribution, 134, *135*
replication crisis in psychology, xii, 71, 73, 135
responses to struggle, retreat and charge. *See* step 4

salience. *See* stereotype threat preconditions
self-esteem, 16–17, 24–25
Sondheim, Stephen, 124
STEM, 93, 99, 113, 115–16, 118, 136
step 1, mindset, fixed and growth, xii, xiii, 8, 47–69, *51*, *53*, *57*, 72–74, 76–81, 108, 117–19, 125, *126*, 128, 135, 137, 141
step 2, goals, performance and learning, xii, 8, 31–38, *34*, 47–48, 51–52, 56, 58, 65–66, 73, 76
step 3, explanations for struggle, ability and effort, xii, 8, 10, 13–16, *15*, 18–20, 22, 25, 27, 29, 31, 36, 47–49, 51–52, 56, 58, 65–66, 73
step 4, responses to struggle, retreat and charge, xi, 5, *6*, 8–11, 13, 17–18, 20, 27, 29, 31, 35, 47–49, 58, 62, 66, 73, 78, 108
stereotype life, 138
stereotypes: age, 89; race/ethnicity, 87–88, *88*, 89–91, 93–94, 115–16, 118–20, *121–22*, 131–32, 136, 138; sex/gender, 87, 89–90, 93–96, 99, 113–16, 118–19, 124, 129, 136, 139; sexuality, 89, 95, 100, 115, 124; socioeconomic status, 89, 93

stereotype threat preconditions, 92–93; #1 salience, xiii, 93, 95–96, *97*, 98, 100, 106, 112–14, 116–17, 121–22, 124–25, *126*, 127–31, 133–34, 136, 138; #2 second-hand belief, 93–96, *97*, 98, 106, 112, 117, 131, 133, 137; #3 skill/interest, 95–98, *97*, 106, 137; #4 difficulty, 96–98, *97*, 106, 137
stereotype threat responses, 92; #1 internal vigilance, 98–100, *101*, 102, 107, 111, 137; #2 external vigilance, 99–100, *101*, 107, 111, 137; #3 stress, 100, *101*, 107, 111, 137
"strategic" thinking, 13–14, 19, 35, 50–52

Talk of the Nation, 105–6
teaching: art, dance, music, theater, 10–11, 23, 28, 41, 65–67; coaching sports, 16, 40, 66–67, *86*, 103, 118; computer science, 113–14; economics, 114–15; English, 6–7, 21, 23, 25, 39–41, 62–63, 67–68, 94–95, 130; ethics, 25, 81; foreign language, 9, 24, 26, 40, 116, 123, 130; history, 3, 17, 22, 23, 28, 40–43, 52, 65–67, 103; K–3, 3, 17, 21, 41, 59, 101, 103, 125; math, 9, 21, 25, 28, 41, 43–44, 57, 65–67, 94–95; science, 3, 17, 23, 26, 37, 41, 60, 65, 67, 101, 103, 116; theology, 65
terminology, 48, 52, 60, 80, 109, 140–41

values affirmation, 133, *135*

wise feedback, 131–32, *132*
working memory, xii, xix, 37, 58, 78, 141; and stereotype threat, 92, 101–4, *104*, 107, 111–12, 133–34, 137

"yet," 28–29, *29*

About the Author

Andrew Watson began high-school teaching in 1988 and has been in or near classrooms ever since.

In 2012, Andrew earned a master's degree in the emerging field of Mind, Brain, and Education at Harvard's Graduate School of Education. Since then, he has worked with thousands of teachers, students, and parents in dozens of K–16 schools—from Cairo to Cleveland, from Tokyo to Texas. He presents regularly at national conferences, including Learning and the Brain and TABS-NAIS Global. For more than two years, he has edited the Learning and the Brain blog.

In his sixteen years as an English teacher, Andrew worked at Concord Academy, Phillips Exeter Summer School, and Loomis Chaffee—where he also served as dean of faculty. He holds an AB from Harvard College and an MA in English literature from Boston University.

Andrew lived in Prague after the Velvet Revolution, working at the Charter 77 Foundation and managing a Beatles tribute band. He currently lives in Somerville, Massachusetts.

Made in the USA
Coppell, TX
04 May 2022

77418459R00102